MISADVENTURE:
MONOLOGUES
AND SHORT PIECES

BY DONALD MARGULIES

★

★

DRAMATISTS
PLAY SERVICE
INC.

MISADVENTURE: MONOLOGUES AND SHORT PIECES
Copyright © 2004, Donald Margulies

All Rights Reserved

For my son, Miles

AUTHOR'S NOTE

Many of the monologues and short pieces contained in this volume were written and developed while the author was a member of The New York Writers Bloc (1977–88), a group to which he is forever indebted.

CONTENTS

MISADVENTURE:
MONOLOGUES
AND SHORT PIECES

NOCTURNE

*Inspired by the collages
of Max Ernst*

NOCTURNE was commissioned by the Center Theatre Group of Los Angeles, Mark Taper Forum.

NOCTURNE was the curtain raiser for *Broken Sleep: Three Plays,* which also included *Broken Sleep* and *July 7, 1994.* Its world premiere took place at the Williamstown Theatre Festival on July 16, 1997. It was directed by Lisa Peterson; the original music was composed by Michael-John LaChiusa; the musical director was Georgia C. Stitt; the set design was by Kathleen Widomski; the lighting design was by Jeffrey Nellis; and the costumes and masks were by Linda Cho. The ensemble included Kate Burton, Tony Campisi, Divina Cook, Adriane Lenox, Paula Newsome and Cotter Smith. The Boy was played by Bryan Hughes.

NOCTURNE

Night. A child's room. A brass bed. A full moon. A chair. A side table on which sits a basin and pitcher. An old-fashioned doll house is on the floor. A title is projected and then fades out:

NOCTURNE

A Boy in blue-and-white striped pajamas, his limbs in haphazard array (arm flung over his head, leg dangling off the bed), is fast asleep. A gleaming, translucent orb rises out of his bed and hovers above him. Title:

A WONDERFUL SURPRISE

The Boy awakens to find the tantalizing object looming above him, sits up, then excitedly stands on the bed to try to take hold of it. He jumps up and down but the orb is elusive; it teases him, continually floating within the Boy's reach, then rising too high to be snatched. He leaps off the bed and follows it around the room. The Boy's hands are outstretched as the orb blows away in a whooshing wind. Title:

ALL ALONE IN THE NIGHT

The Boy looks around the room. A little spooked, he clutches his stuffed rabbit and sits in the chair. The lights inside the doll house suddenly go on, casting shadows on the wall. The Boy turns his attention to the house and goes to it. He sits on the floor and plays, moving doll-like figures around the rooms. Title:

THE SKY CRACKS OPEN

There is a sudden crash of thunder and bursts of white lightning. The frightened Boy runs to the doorway and silently calls: "Mama!

11

Daddy!" (We hear his recorded voice on tape.) He runs back to his bed and hides under his pillow. Title:

I HEAR MONSTERS WHISPERING

A Monster wearing a dark suit and lizard mask crawls out from under the bed. (These Monsters walk like humans, on two feet.) The Boy peers from behind his pillow watching the Lizard walk about, exploring the room. A second Monster, also in a suit and wearing an alligator mask, comes out holding an alligator-skin doctor's bag and joins him. Insidiously, they pick up the Boy's toys and inspect them as if they're foreign objects, consulting with one another in an eerie whisper, repeating: "Hush." The Monsters put various playthings into the bag. The Boy is fearful at first, then curious, then incensed that the Monsters are taking his things without his permission. As the creatures are about to walk out the door, the Boy stands up in bed and shouts: "Hey!" The Monsters are startled; their green eyes light up when they see him. Title:

UH OH!

The Monsters take chase after the Boy, who runs around the room. Finally, the Boy dashes under the bed but the Lizard pulls him out by his foot. The Alligator brandishes a gleaming dagger and raises it to strike. The struggling Boy is about to scream but the Lizard covers his mouth. The Monsters' hushing continues. Title:

A FLUTTERING OF WINGS

A fluttering sound precedes the entrance of two Birds, both wearing long Victorian dresses with bustles. Their appearance reprieves the Boy. The Birds and the Monsters fight over the Boy, who is passed around from creature to creature. The squawking Birds succeed in driving the Monsters out the door. The Birds hold on to the Boy and prepare to take off with him in tow. Title:

I AM STOLEN!

The terrified Boy opens his mouth to scream; he makes no sound but we hear a piercing, piteous wail (made by his Mother offstage) as he's whisked away by the Birds. The sound of wings flapping fades as he vanishes. The wailing continues as the Boy's barefoot, grief-stricken Mother, dressed in a nightgown, her long tresses flowing wildly, runs into the room gesturing dolefully with her hands, followed closely by the Boy's somber Father, also barefoot, wearing a smoking jacket and holding a lit candle. Title:

AN EMPTY BED

The Mother sobs-sings a mournful melody as the Father tries to console her and get her to sit in the chair, while he sorrowfully caresses the lost Boy's blanket. But the Mother is too agitated to be still. She goes to the Father. He attempts to calm her but she makes harsh sounds of recrimination and pummels him with her fists. He takes hold of her hands, stopping her. She relents and lets him hold her in his arms. In the flickering candlelight, their lulling swaying becomes a tango of grief. The Boy appears briefly, high above the wall. He sees his parents dancing, then dips out of view. There is a knock at the door. The Boy's parents stand together in trepidation. Title:

WHO IS AT THE DOOR?

A Policeman in a long overcoat, wearing a handsome lion's head, appears in the doorway. The Mother gasps, puts her hand over her mouth. The Father wraps his arm around her. In a moment, the Boy peers from behind the Policeman. The Mother opens her arms to embrace him. The grateful Father goes to shake the Policeman's hand. The Policeman leaves. The Boy enjoys an emotional reunion with his parents. They mime animated conversation. Title:

I TELL THEM ABOUT MY ADVENTURE
AND HOW I GOT TO RIDE IN A POLICE CAR

But it's time to go back to sleep. The Mother puts him in bed and tucks him in. She hums a lullaby and kisses him. The Father kisses him, too, and goes. The Mother follows, glancing back at the Boy before she exits. The Boy appears to have fallen back asleep, but in a moment, he sits up in bed, squirrels under his covers and emerges with — a translucent orb! Smiling in wonder, he holds it in his hands. The object begins to hover just above his hands. Title:

I HAVE MY PRIZE!

The room is in darkness. Title:

THE END

LUNA PARK

Inspired by the short story
"In Dreams Begin Responsibilities"
by Delmore Schwartz

In memory of my grandparents,
Rose and Jack Bender

LUNA PARK was commissioned and produced by New York's Jewish Repertory Theatre (Ran Avni, Artistic Director) on February 6, 1982, as one-half of "Delmore: An Evening of Two One-Act Plays," which included *Shenandoah* by Delmore Schwartz. It was directed by Florence Stanley; the set design was by Ken Rothchild; the lighting design was by Carol B. Sealey; the sound design was by Andrew Howard; and the costumes were by Linda Vigdor. The cast was as follows:

ROSE, USHER,
VOICE OF GRANDMOTHER .... Barbara Glenn Gordon
DELMORE, GRANDFATHER, MAN
WALKING DOG, MAN FEEDING PIGEONS,
MERRY-GO-ROUND OPERATOR, WAITER,
PHOTOGRAPHER, FORTUNE TELLER .... Willie Reale
YOUNG ROSE .... Susan Merson
HARRY .... David Wohl

CHARACTERS

ACTOR #1 (early twenties):
  DELMORE, GRANDFATHER, MAN
  WALKING DOG, MAN FEEDING PIGEONS,
  MERRY-GO-ROUND OPERATOR, WAITER,
  PHOTOGRAPHER, FORTUNE TELLER

ACTOR #2 (about twenty-nine):
  HARRY

ACTRESS #1 (late forties):
  ROSE, USHER, VOICE OF
  GRANDMOTHER

ACTRESS #2 (early twenties):
  YOUNG ROSE

TIME AND PLACE

The Prologue and Epilogue are set in the kitchen of the Schwartz apartment in New York City in December 1934.

The dream portion of the play begins in a movie theatre; the "film" which unfolds takes place in Brooklyn, primarily parts of Coney Island. The time is June 1909.

LUNA PARK

PROLOGUE

The time is December 1934. Delmore sits at the kitchen table reading. His mother, Rose, stands at the sink washing dishes; she raises her voice to be heard over the running water. Her back is to him, his chair is turned away from her. Long silence. Delmore yawns.

ROSE. So you thinking it over what I said? *(Pause.)* Thinking?
DELMORE. *(Doesn't look up from his book.)* Uh-huh.
ROSE. I know I told you "anything." I don't mean *any*thing. Believe me, it would be very nice if I could say "anything" and mean "*any*thing" but this is the way with the world today. I'm very sorry. *(Scraping a dish into the trash.)* How come you didn't touch your carrots?
DELMORE. I don't like carrots.
ROSE. Since when?
DELMORE. I've never liked carrots. I don't think I've ever really eaten carrots.
ROSE. Why didn't you tell me?
DELMORE. Why didn't you know? *(Pause.)*
ROSE. I can't keep track of everything. I'm very sorry. I got a lot on my mind. *(A beat.)* Should I save the carrots? *(She puts her hand in the garbage bag ready to retrieve them.)* Huh?
DELMORE. If you want them, save them. I'm not going to eat them.
ROSE. *(Thinks for a second.)* Oh, I'll live without the carrots. I feel terrible. You know I don't like putting into the garbage what should go into your mouth. *(A beat, then to herself.)* Damn the

21

carrots. *(To Delmore, but she doesn't look at him.)* Did you know that if you eat too many carrots your eyes turn yellow? Yes. Isn't that something? Who would believe something like that? *(Pause.)* Next time tell me what you like instead of into the garbage. *(Pause.)* I know what you could use and it makes a lot of sense: a scarf. How about a scarf of some kind? *(Delmore shrugs but she doesn't see him.)* Answer me.

DELMORE. I said I don't care!

ROSE. I didn't hear you, excuse me. *(Pause.)* I'm sorry about the dinner. *(Pause.)* Did you hear me?

DELMORE. Don't apologize.

ROSE. I didn't know how you feel about carrots, I'm sorry, it slipped my mind. I did what I could with the dinner.

DELMORE. It was a fine dinner.

ROSE. No. There's just so much I can do with what I got. Look, if your father had stayed with his wife and family … if your father was the responsible gentleman … hadn't thrown himself into a grave and taken every penny with him, there at least would have been a decent brisket on the table. And a cake! A birthday cake. With your name on it in sugar icing.

DELMORE. I don't care for cake.

ROSE. Who you kidding you don't care for cake. You love cake. A cake would've been perfect. A cake would've been wonderful. Twenty-one is a big deal. I tried to make you a slightly special supper. I'm sorry about the brisket. I asked for a reasonable-looking brisket. I told him, I can't pay you much but give me the most reasonable cut you got. Sure, Rose. So, what does he give me? Uch, fatty, terrible.

DELMORE. It was all right, Ma, it was all right.

ROSE. It was not all right. It was a terrible brisket. Fatty fatty. Sure, Rose, I believed him. I took his word. He's not an honest man but stupid Rose, I believed him. I should've known better than to trust that man but, oh, he has charm, a sense of humor. I feel so stupid I could spit. "You call that lean?" I says. "It's lean, it's lean," he says, "what do you want, bones?" Damn him! *(Long pause.)* And he charges me an arm and a leg. For this terrible disgusting fatty unreasonable brisket. *Goniff. (Delmore stands, heads for the doorway.)* Where you going?

DELMORE. I, I think I'll read in bed.

ROSE. So you can burn up more electricity killing your eyes? Burning electricity costs money. You're not the son of Rockefeller no more I hate to tell you …

DELMORE. *(Approaching the door.)* Good night.

ROSE. Stay till I finish up. So you'll read in here, why burn another bulb when you got this one going? Stay, sit, read. *(A beat. Delmore relents.)* Think over what you want for your birthday. Sit and think. You're smart, I'm sure you'll think of something. You got a big brain in there, what do you want? *(Delmore leans on the edge of the table.)* What?

DELMORE. There's a book I want. *(Pause. Rose stops what she's doing and looks at him.)*

ROSE. A book? *(Pause.)* You're making a joke.

DELMORE. No I'm not.

ROSE. A book is very smart.

DELMORE. You asked me what I wanted!

ROSE. Yeah, but a book?! A book is just what you need. You must have twenty-*five* books in there! A book is not something you can wrap around your neck when the wind hits you like ice!

DELMORE. I don't want anything!

ROSE. But I want to *give* you something. This is no regular birthday … you can *vote* now. Isn't that wonderful? You can vote for the President of the United States! *(As she speaks, Delmore notices a tear in her sweater. A beat.)* What.

DELMORE. *(Surprised.)* Your sweater is ripped.

ROSE. *(Tries to hide it.)* It's nothing.

DELMORE. Why haven't you sewn it?

ROSE. Never mind.

DELMORE. Why don't you mend it? It's in the seam …

ROSE. I'll live with it. Don't worry about it. *(She takes off the sweater, throws it over a chair.)*

DELMORE. The slightest tear, the smallest pull of a thread, and you'd be stitching it right up. This is so unlike you.

ROSE. *(Welling up with tears; yells.)* This *isn't* unlike me! This *is* me! *(She cries.)* This is me … *(Pause. Delmore watches her, uncertain of what to do.)*

DELMORE. I'll get your basket so you can fix it. *(He starts to go.)*

ROSE. *(Composing herself.)* No. Forget about it. The sweater is shot. It kept me warm enough years. It's shot, it's not worth it, don't worry about it, it's not your problem. *(She blows her nose.)* There's just so much I can do with what I got. I'm sorry if you don't like it.

DELMORE. I'm not criticizing you.

ROSE. *(Again, in tears.)* Yes you are! Look how you look at me! You look at me like I got a disease! Stop it!

DELMORE. *(Turns away from her.)* I'm just trying to understand.

ROSE. What, Professor? What don't you understand?

DELMORE. I don't know how we got here, Ma. How'd this happen?

ROSE. This isn't what I had in mind. Believe me. I had other plans. *(She cries. Delmore tries to comfort her but cannot.)* Leave me now. Leave me. Go, sleep. When you wake up, you'll be twenty-one. Go. *(Delmore hesitates, then exits. Pause, then to herself.)* If only there was a cake ... *(Fade out. Lights up. Delmore in his bedroom. He goes to a phonograph and turns on a record. Rose's faint sobs meld into a scratchy recording of a Haydn string quartet. Delmore paces the room as he undresses and gets into his pajamas. He examines himself in a mirror for a while. Soon he settles into bed with a book. He dozes off. A shift in the lighting indicates passage of time. Delmore is in a deep sleep. We hear the needle of the phonograph skipping and the amplified sound of heavy restful breathing. Fade out. The sounds continue in the darkness.)*

SCENE ONE

As a flashlight pierces the darkness, there is a surge of organ music, the kind played in movie palaces in the early part of the century. The stage is clear except for a movie theatre seat which is situated at rear center, facing the audience. The flashlight is held by an Usher, who enters showing Delmore to his seat. The Usher is played by Rose. She wears the sweater Rose wore in the Prologue. Delmore is barefoot and wearing his pajamas. The Usher speaks in an exaggerated sibilant whisper.

USHER. Shhh ... You just made it. Sit still. Don't make a sound. *(The sound of a movie projector is heard. A beam of flickering light is shone on the audience from behind Delmore.)* It's starting. *(Young Rose enters from stage right and faces the audience.)* Look what a beauty your mother was ... *(The Usher begins to exit stage right. Harry enters, left, and faces the audience.)* And there *he* is ... *(Harry jingles the change in his pocket.)* Yeah, that's him ... *(The Usher stands near Young Rose. She takes off her sweater; to Delmore.)* It's June 12, 1909. A Sunday. A beautiful day in Brooklyn. A chill is in the air. *(The Usher drapes the sweater over Young Rose's shoulders.)* Now shush and shut up and watch the movie. *(The Usher exits. The sound of the projector becomes louder, the flickering lights brighter. In a beat, Delmore runs offstage. Door chimes. Pause. Door chimes again. Rose is now heard as the offstage voice of her own mother, Delmore's Grandmother.)*
GRANDMOTHER'S VOICE. Just a second ... Joseph, get the door. *(Door chimes again.)* Joseph! Please! I'm washing dishes ...
GRANDFATHER'S VOICE. *(Spoken by Delmore.)* Just a second! *(Lights up. Harry waits to be admitted to the home of Delmore's grandparents. Harry fixes his necktie and takes a deep breath. In a beat, Delmore hurriedly enters as his own Grandfather. He wipes his mouth with a napkin, clears his throat, then opens the front door.)*
GRANDFATHER. Oh! Mr. Schwartz ... *(Grandfather wipes his hands thoroughly with his napkin.)*

HARRY. Mr. Nathanson ... you're eating. *(Grandfather takes Harry's hand, shakes it.)*
GRANDFATHER. No, Mr. Schwartz, I'm shaking your hand. Come in.
HARRY. *(Fumbling with his watch.)* I thought I planned it perfect. I told Rose "one." Please, eat, make believe I'm not here.
GRANDMOTHER'S VOICE. Joseph, who is it?
GRANDFATHER. *(Calls to her.)* It's Harry Schwartz.
HARRY. *(Calls.)* Hello, Mrs. Nathanson.
GRANDMOTHER'S VOICE. Oh, hello, Mr. Schwartz. It's one o'clock already?
HARRY and GRANDFATHER. No, no ...
GRANDFATHER. He's a couple minutes early.
HARRY. I'm a little early.
GRANDMOTHER'S VOICE. You're a little bit early I think.
HARRY. Yes. So it seems.
GRANDFATHER. Relax, Mr. Schwartz.
HARRY. Please, Mr. Nathanson, go eat.
GRANDFATHER. I ate, relax. Are you uncomfortable or something, Mr. Schwartz?
HARRY. No ...
GRANDMOTHER'S VOICE. Is he uncomfortable or something?
HARRY. *(Calls.)* No.
GRANDMOTHER'S VOICE. Tell him to sit down.
GRANDFATHER. Sit down, Mr. Schwartz. *(Harry and Grandfather sit.)*
HARRY. Please, I didn't mean to interrupt your meal ...
GRANDFATHER. You didn't interrupt.
GRANDMOTHER'S VOICE. Is he hungry?
HARRY. No ...
GRANDFATHER. He says no.
GRANDMOTHER'S VOICE. Mr. Schwartz, feel like nibbling on a little brisket?
HARRY. No, thank you ...
GRANDMOTHER'S VOICE. It's a wonderful lean brisket.
HARRY. So, where *is* Rose?
GRANDFATHER. Upstairs. Staring in the mirror.
HARRY. Oh, I see. *(Harry and Grandfather share a knowing laugh.)*

GRANDFATHER. You know how Rose is, making sure everything is just so.

HARRY. Yes ... *(Pause.)*

GRANDFATHER. So, Mr. Schwartz ... Tell me: How was traveling from New York?

HARRY. Oh, I had an exceptionally nice walk.

GRANDFATHER. You *walked,* Mr. Schwartz?

GRANDMOTHER'S VOICE. What, Joseph?

GRANDFATHER. *(Calls.)* Mr. Schwartz walked, he says.

GRANDMOTHER'S VOICE. He walked?! Oh my God! All the way to Brooklyn?

HARRY. Yes ...

GRANDMOTHER'S VOICE. That's some distance!

HARRY. Yes ...

GRANDMOTHER'S VOICE. Across the bridge and everything?

HARRY. Yes ...

GRANDMOTHER'S VOICE. My God!

HARRY. I love to walk. Walking is exceptional exercise.

GRANDMOTHER'S VOICE. What an ambitious young man ...

GRANDFATHER. Yes, what an ambitious young man!

HARRY. And what an exceptional day for a walk!

GRANDFATHER. Perfect.

HARRY. Yes.

GRANDFATHER. A perfect day for a walk. A perfect day all around.

HARRY. Yes. And what a sight from the bridge: the Statue of Liberty, her lantern high in the blue, blue sky, the stars and stripes blowing in the breeze! *(Harry and Grandfather sigh reverently.)*

GRANDMOTHER'S VOICE. What he say, Joseph?

GRANDFATHER. The Statue of Liberty! The stars and stripes! *(We hear Grandmother also sigh.)*

GRANDMOTHER'S VOICE. You picked a beautiful day for a walk, Mr. Schwartz.

HARRY. Walking lets me clear my head, gives me a chance to smoke some expensive cigars.

GRANDMOTHER'S VOICE. You smoke cigars, Mr. Schwartz?

HARRY. Yes.

GRANDMOTHER'S VOICE. And why not?! If you enjoy it ...

GRANDFATHER. Would you like a cigar, Mr. Schwartz?

GRANDMOTHER'S VOICE. Joseph, if you're going to start with the cigar smoke, open the window.

HARRY. Would *you* like a cigar, Mr. Nathanson? *(Harry takes two cigars from the inside pocket of his jacket.)*

GRANDFATHER. *(Extends a cigar to Harry.)* No, take one of mine, young man.

HARRY. These cigars are very, very expensive, Mr. Nathanson, and very, very high quality. Please take one.

GRANDFATHER. My cigar is a fine cigar, Mr. Schwartz.

HARRY. Yes, but mine are from Havana, Cuba. *(A beat. Grandfather hesitates, then takes Harry's cigar. They sit silently for a little while as they light their cigars.)*

GRANDFATHER. So ... how's business, Mr. Schwartz?

HARRY. You're asking the right person about business.

GRANDFATHER. Oh, yes? *(Harry sits forward in his chair and speaks confidentially to Grandfather:)*

HARRY. Just between you and me, Mr. Nathanson, I'll let you in on a little secret: Business is doing very nice ... *(Grasps Grandfather's hand for emphasis.)* *Very* nice.

GRANDFATHER. Good for you.

HARRY. And *this* week, Mr. Nathanson, I'm not embarrassed to tell you ... This week business was exceptional.

GRANDFATHER. Good.

HARRY. Better than ever.

GRANDFATHER. *Mazel tov.*

HARRY. Better even than *last* week.

GRANDFATHER. Good!

HARRY. And last week I thought things couldn't be better. *(During this last line, Young Rose enters. She is wearing the cardigan that was draped over her shoulders earlier by the elder Rose. Harry is made momentarily uneasy by her presence, uncertain whether to greet her or continue his conversation with Grandfather. Young Rose stands timidly, waiting to be acknowledged.)* But *this* week, Mr. Nathanson, through the roof! *(Harry laughs. Grandfather joins him briefly. Young Rose smiles broadly but doesn't understand the context of the laughter. When the joke dies down, there is an uncomfortable pause. Then Harry stands clumsily and greets her.)* Hello.

YOUNG ROSE. *(Hereafter referred to as Rose.)* Hello. *(Pause.)*

HARRY. Hello, Rose.

ROSE. Hello, Harry. *(Grandfather begins to cough from the cigar smoke. To Grandfather:)* Are you all right? *(Grandfather nods his head while choking.)*

GRANDMOTHER'S VOICE. Joseph, are you coughing? I told you open the window! *(Pause. Grandfather's seizure stops.)*

HARRY. So, Rose, are you ready for Coney Island?

GRANDFATHER. Coney Island? Is that where you're taking Rose, Mr. Schwartz?

HARRY. Yes.

GRANDFATHER. *(Joking.)* I'd love to go to Coney Island. What if I came along? *(Harry and Rose laugh briefly. Silence.)*

HARRY. *(To Rose.)* Ready?

ROSE. Yes, Harry.

HARRY. *(Refers to her sweater.)* You don't need that.

ROSE. I don't?

HARRY. It's a beautiful day.

ROSE. But, still, I might get cold.

HARRY. Nah …

ROSE. There's a chill in the air I think.

HARRY. No, this is a day you just want to breathe, you don't want clothing to get in the way between you and the air.

ROSE. But it might get chilly.

HARRY. It's like summer, Rose, I promise you. The sun is shining and hot.

GRANDFATHER. Rose, Mr. Schwartz says you can do without the sweater. *(Rose looks at Grandfather, then at Harry. In a beat, she takes the sweater off her shoulders and holds it.)*

HARRY. What an exceptional dress you have on, Rose.

ROSE. Thank you.

HARRY. Look at you! Why would you want to cover up such a beautiful dress? *(Pause. Rose folds the sweater over the back of a chair. Looking at Rose.)* Do you want to know something, Mr. Nathanson?

GRANDFATHER. What?

HARRY. *Your* daughter and *my* business have something in common.

GRANDFATHER. Oh, yes?

HARRY. *(Still looking at Rose.)* Yes. They're both looking extremely exceptional. *(Rose giggles. Silence. Tableau: Harry is facing Rose, who has turned away in embarrassment. Grandfather strokes his chin as he scrutinizes the couple. Lights begin to fade out except for spots on the faces of Rose, Harry and Grandfather. Fade out. Sound of rustling leaves is heard in the darkness.)*

SCENE TWO

A tree-lined street in Brooklyn. Ocean Parkway. Rose and Harry enter from the right and slowly stroll across the stage. Delmore, disguised as a man walking a dog, enters from the left. He eavesdrops on Rose and Harry in mid-conversation.

ROSE. What was that word?
HARRY. Exceptional?
ROSE. Yes. Exceptional. That's what this girl is. She got everything going for her. She's exceptional pretty, got a good head on her shoulders, good taste in clothes, and the kind of smile … her face brightens everybody's day!
HARRY. Ugh.
ROSE. On the outside she looks happy, but on the inside she's not really happy.
HARRY. Of course.
ROSE. All she does is hope that the man of her dreams will come along.
HARRY. Naturally.
ROSE. And then she meets George.
HARRY. Ah! George!
ROSE. She wants to marry George and have children and live in a lovely place, not too big, not too small.
HARRY. How long is this book? *(A beat. They stop walking. Rose is embarrassed.)* So go on. *(Pause.)* Tell me: What happens to this exceptional girl and what's-his-name?

30

ROSE. George.

HARRY. George.

ROSE. Like George Washington. *(Says "Vashington.")*

HARRY. Well? …

ROSE. To her, George is the most wonderful man in the world. But George practically doesn't know she's alive. He always has an eye on the girls (if you know what I mean), but she decides to wait until he comes to his senses and see that *she* is the only woman who will ever really love him.

HARRY. *(Feigned concern.)* Hmm …

ROSE. And then they see each other at the square dance. *(She says "skvair dence.")*

HARRY. Where?

ROSE. Square dance? *(She suggests the dance with her hands.)*

HARRY. *(Not really understanding.)* Oh. *(A beat. He takes hold of Rose and gently dances with her, to her surprise.)* And George dances with her … and then what?

ROSE. *(Through giggles, still dancing.)* George dances with her … and the music plays … and he spins her around …

HARRY. Like this? *(Spins her around quickly.)*

ROSE. *(Caught up in the excitement.)* Yes! And they look into each other's eyes … *(Suddenly, Harry stops dancing. He has stepped in droppings left by Delmore's "dog." He angrily looks at Delmore, who stands nearby; Delmore shrugs an apology. Harry scrapes his shoe on the sidewalk while Rose looks on, bemused but disappointed that the dance ended so abruptly. Rose giggles nervously. Pause. Harry continues to scrape his shoe against the pavement.)* You should read the way the writer writes it. It made me cry. He did some job, that writer. What a way with words.

HARRY. So George and this girl, they live happily ever after, huh?

ROSE. Well, no.

HARRY. No?

ROSE. Well, they fall in love and get married and for a little while they're happy. And they have children. And then they trick each other.

HARRY. Trick?

ROSE. Fool. They fool each other. They make things up. They don't tell the truth. They trick each other.

31

HARRY. Lies.

ROSE. Yes. Little lies. Little lies that get bigger and bigger, until she can't look at George in the eye no more. *(They briefly make eye contact but turn away from one another. A depressed silence.)*

HARRY. What are you so sad about? It's just a silly book!

ROSE. Do you think so?

HARRY. I don't know what good books are if they make people sad. We're going to Coney Island! I promise you'll forget all about George and this silly girl ...

ROSE. A walk on the boardwalk would be nice ...

HARRY. And Luna Park! What about Luna Park!?

ROSE. No ...

HARRY. I'll take you there, Rose ...

ROSE. Not today, thank you. Not today Luna Park. Not that class of people and all that crazy noise and light. No, some other time Luna Park.

HARRY. Whatever you want, Rose. I promise. Forget about that sad silly book ... we're going to Coney Island! *(Rose and Harry resume walking across the stage. Tableau: They're frozen in mid-step. Rose looks at Harry, whose expression is that of uncertainty. Delmore, as the man walking a dog, glances over his shoulder at them. Lights fade except for three lingering spots on their faces. Fade out. The sound of the ocean is heard in the darkness.)*

SCENE THREE

On the boardwalk in Coney Island. Rose and Harry are leaning on the railing watching the ocean. Delmore stands nearby, at another segment of railing, disguised in unkempt clothing as a man tossing crumbs to pigeons.

HARRY. Ah! Take a whiff of that sea air!

ROSE. Yes.

HARRY. Smell it. Take a deep breath and smell it.

ROSE. *(Inhales; then.)* Yes.

HARRY. No, really smell it. Feel it fill your head. *(He instructs her how to inhale. She laughs, then he does, too. Long silence.)* This is the best air you could breathe.

ROSE. It's very good for you.

HARRY. What?

ROSE. It's good for you, this air.

HARRY. The best. It's good for the lungs and the whole internal system. *(Pause.)* I believe in health.

ROSE. Health is the most important thing, yes. Even more than having money. All I want is health.

HARRY. That's all.

ROSE. *(After a beat.)* And money. *(They laugh. Pause.)*

HARRY. I believe in things that are good for you. *(Takes a cigar from his inside pocket and lights it.)* Some people don't know what good is.

ROSE. Fruit for instance.

HARRY. Yes, fruit. Also, vegetables. *(He says "veg-e-tables.")*

ROSE. Spinach …

HARRY. I don't care for spinach.

ROSE. Oh. Peas, string beans …

HARRY. Carrots …

ROSE. Carrots I like very much. I could eat carrots every day.

HARRY. Don't eat too many carrots.

ROSE. Why?

HARRY. Too much is no good for you.

ROSE. Why?

HARRY. It does something to your eyes.

ROSE. My *eyes?*

HARRY. Too many carrots make your eyes turn yellow.

ROSE. You're making a joke …

HARRY. No, I'm telling the truth: Your eyes will turn yellow if you eat too many carrots.

ROSE. You're trying to fool me …

HARRY. Why would I fool you?

ROSE. I think you're making a joke.

HARRY. Young lady, I am not making a joke. I'm telling you a scientific fact: Too many carrots in your system and your eyes will turn yellow.

ROSE. But my eyes are practically black, how can they go from black to yellow?

HARRY. *(His patience flagging.)* The white part *around* your eyes …

ROSE. Oh. *(Pause.)* Still, I don't believe you.

HARRY. Why would I lie about something like this?

ROSE. To fool me.

HARRY. No, I wouldn't do that.

ROSE. Well, I still think this business about carrots is a trick. You want me to believe it but I can't.

HARRY. Then believe what you wish. *(A disturbed silence. They lean on the railing and look at the ocean, although they're preoccupied. Delmore, who has eavesdropped on them all along, continues to toss crumbs to pigeons. Trying to lighten things up.)* Peanuts?

ROSE. What?

HARRY. Peanuts?

ROSE. *(A beat.)* I don't understand …

HARRY. *(Hiding his exasperation.)* Would you like me to get you some peanuts? *(A beat.)* Peanuts are good for you. You can eat all you want, your eyes won't change color.

ROSE. *(Charmed.)* All right.

HARRY. I'll be right back. *(Rose nods. Harry exits. Rose leans on the railing and looks at the ocean impassively. The weather begins to change; the lighting dims and sounds of the wind and waves grow intense. Rose crosses her arms and holds herself to keep warm. She looks around for Harry but doesn't see him.)*

DELMORE. *(As the man feeding pigeons.)* The tide is changing.

ROSE. *(Realizes he's talking to her.)* What?

DELMORE. The tide. Do you hear it? It's getting rougher. *(A beat. Rose doesn't know what to make of him.)* Do you see how the waves somersault? Roll and crack, roll and crack … Listen to it. *(Rose has begun to chatter from the cold. She looks for Harry again.)* Look at the ocean!

ROSE. *(Uncomfortably.)* Very nice.

DELMORE. *(Amused by her casual response.)* Very nice? *(A beat. He notices she's shivering.)* Your teeth are chattering …

ROSE. Please go away.

DELMORE. Don't you have a sweater to put on? *(Harry enters*

34

with a bag of peanuts.)

ROSE. Harry ... *(Rose giggles nervously and whispers.)* Harry, there's a crazy man over there ... *(Harry looks at Delmore, then protectively leads Rose a few feet away.)*

DELMORE. I was just pointing out the beauty of the ocean ...

HARRY. Never mind, mister.

DELMORE. ... Look at it! It's right in front of your eyes!

ROSE. *(Quietly, to Harry.)* Harry, please, can we go...?

HARRY. We were here first, we're not going anywhere.

ROSE. *(Shivering.)* Please ...

HARRY. We had this spot first.

ROSE. But the wind is like ice.

DELMORE. The tide is changing.

HARRY. It's an exceptional day, enjoy it.

DELMORE. She's freezing.

HARRY. *(The fight escalates.)* That's none of your business, mister.

DELMORE. How can you let her stand there shivering?

ROSE. Harry, please ...

HARRY. *(Overlapping.)* Mister, butt out!

DELMORE. Give her your jacket. Don't let her stand there shaking ...

HARRY. Don't tell me what to do ...

DELMORE. You *look* like a responsible gentleman ... *(Harry is about to hit him. Rose restrains him.)*

ROSE. Harry, please, I don't want to stand here no more.

HARRY. It's a matter of principle, Rose.

ROSE. But let's go inside someplace.

DELMORE. Give her your jacket at least.

HARRY. Mister ...

ROSE. Harry ...

HARRY. *(Begins to take off his jacket.)* Here.

ROSE. No.

HARRY. Put it on. You won't be cold.

ROSE. I don't want it.

HARRY. You said you were cold.

ROSE. I don't want your jacket. If you had let me take my sweater, everything would be fine.

HARRY. Oh, so this is *my* fault? You didn't have to listen to me ...

ROSE. But you promised me I wouldn't need it!

HARRY. I'm very sorry! I'm not the *Farmer's Almanac!*

DELMORE. Don't be a fool, take her inside. *(Harry is enraged again and points his finger pugnaciously at Delmore.)*

ROSE. Harry, let's go ...

HARRY. *(Looking at Delmore.)* Of course, Rose. *(He takes her arm and begins to lead her off.)* Whatever you like. *(Harry crumples the bag of peanuts and tosses it behind him. Delmore picks up the bag and tosses peanuts to the birds. Tableau: Rose and Harry in mid-step. Only their backs are visible [their exit is not quite complete] but Harry has turned his head for a final look at Delmore. Lights begin to fade except for three spots on their faces. Fade out. A sudden burst of calliope music is heard in the darkness.)*

SCENE FOUR

On a merry-go-round. Rose and Harry move in such a way as to suggest the rotation of a carousel. Perhaps they're holding wooden horses' heads. Delmore, disguised as the merry-go-round operator, is tending to the rings which the riders try to grasp. The riders' movement becomes faster, the music louder, and their moods more exultant. Harry laughs. Rose giggles uncontrollably. They make repeated grabs for rings; Delmore fixes it so that Harry consistently gets them and Rose always misses. The music accelerates until it ends abruptly in a sour screech. Silence. Blackout. The sound of the ocean is heard in the darkness.

SCENE FIVE

A restaurant on the boardwalk. Rose and Harry are seated at a table finishing dinner. Sound of distant violin.

HARRY. So…?
ROSE. Wonderful.
HARRY. Yes?
ROSE. Exceptional.
HARRY. What did I tell you? Didn't I promise you?
ROSE. Yes.
HARRY. I didn't lie when I said this is the best restaurant in Coney Island.
ROSE. No.
HARRY. This is the best.
ROSE. So you said. *(A beat.)* Thank you.
HARRY. Don't thank me. It's my pleasure. It gives me pleasure to take you to the best restaurant.
ROSE. *(Shyly.)* Thank you.
HARRY. Don't thank me. *(A beat.)* You should've ordered the lobster. *(Delmore, disguised as a waiter, enters during above and stands by his station.)*
ROSE. But I liked the fish …
HARRY. *(Overlapping.)* I saw your face when you saw the price. You don't have to be shy with me, Rose. As long as you're with Harry Schwartz, you can have a-ny-thing you want. *(A short but pregnant pause.)* Rose.
ROSE. Yes, Harry?
HARRY. Rose … *(Delmore breaks the tense moment by coming between them with a pitcher of water. He refills their glasses.)*
DELMORE. Would you like to see dessert menus? *(Rose shakes her head no to Harry. A beat.)*
HARRY. *(To Delmore.)* Yes. Yes, please. *(To Rose.)* Their desserts are outta this world. *(Delmore hands a menu to Rose; she refuses it.*

Harry takes his.) Have something.

ROSE. I don't want nothing.

DELMORE. Today's special dessert is chocolate layer cake.

HARRY. *(For Rose's benefit.)* That sounds good.

DELMORE. It's our specialty.

HARRY. *(To Rose.)* It's their specialty.

ROSE. *(Growing uncomfortable.)* Don't worry about me.

HARRY. *(Looking over the menu.)* How about orange sherbet?

ROSE. No.

HARRY. *(To Delmore.)* A very particular young lady. *(Delmore chuckles briefly with Harry; Rose is annoyed and embarrassed.)*

ROSE. Okay I'll have the sherbet.

HARRY. Good.

DELMORE. *(To Rose.)* Are you sure you want the sherbet? There isn't much to it.

ROSE. Yes …

DELMORE. It's not much of a portion. It's sweet, but over very quickly. Have the chocolate layer cake.

ROSE. No. I'll have the sherbet.

DELMORE. The chocolate layer cake is rich and delicious. And the portion is impressive.

ROSE. No. The sherbet, please. *(A beat.)*

DELMORE. All right.

HARRY. Strawberry cheesecake. *(Harry closes the menu, returns it to Delmore.)*

DELMORE. *(Repeats to himself.)* Strawberry cheesecake. Coffee? *(Harry looks to Rose.)*

ROSE. *(To Harry.)* Tea.

HARRY. *(To Delmore.)* Two teas, please. *(Delmore nods, begins to exit. Harry calls after him.)* In a glass. *(Delmore exits. Pause.)*

ROSE. Finish what you were saying.

HARRY. Saying?

ROSE. Before. You said to me, as long as I'm with Harry Schwartz …

HARRY. *(A beat.)* Oh. Yes. *(Pause.)* You know, Rose, I go for the finer things in life …

ROSE. I do, too, Harry.

HARRY. An expensive cigar at my fingertips, nice material on my

38

back …

ROSE. Yes …

HARRY. Good food in my stomach …

ROSE. Yes … *(Romantic music slowly begins to build in intensity.)*

HARRY. A comfortable place to live …

ROSE. … not too big, not too small …

HARRY. … that's got heat when it's snowing, and maybe a bungalow by the ocean where you can cool off when everybody else sweats …

ROSE. *(An excited giggle.)* Yes …

HARRY. I earned these things, Rose. I *earned* them.

ROSE. And you should be proud of yourself.

HARRY. I *am* proud of myself. Why shouldn't I be proud of myself? I've come a long way since I got off the boat: a thirteen-year-old kid with big eyes and skinny ribs and holes in his pockets. *(Delmore enters carrying a tray, sets it down.)* America's been good to me, Rose, and now I think it's time to settle down … *(The music, which had begun to surge, stops abruptly when Delmore interrupts; he stands between them with the dessert plates in his hands: plain cheesecake and chocolate layer cake.)*

DELMORE. *(Crassly.)* Okay, who's got the chocolate layer cake?

HARRY. *(A beat.)* Neither of us.

DELMORE. Are you sure?

HARRY. *(Losing patience.)* I ordered the *straw*berry cheesecake and the young lady is having the sherbet.

DELMORE. I was mistaken.

HARRY. Yes.

delmore *(To Rose.)* Would you like it now that I've brought it?

HARRY. No she would not. And I wanted *straw*berry cheesecake.

DELMORE. Terribly sorry. *(Delmore exits. Pause.)*

ROSE. Go on, Harry.

HARRY. What was I saying?

ROSE. You were talking about settling down?

HARRY. Oh, yes. Settling down. *(The romantic music begins to build once more.)* You know, Rose, in the real estate game you get to see a lot of people settle down. That definitely has its rewards (in more ways than one, if you know what I mean). It's nice to see people planting roots and it's also nice earning a very handsome living. But, lately, it does something to me, Rose … it does something inside of me seeing these men (my age and even younger) with their pretty wives and children …

ROSE. Children?

HARRY. … building homes for themselves on land *I* sold them. It does something to me. I want that, too. After all, I'm twenty-nine years old, almost thirty, and it's time already. *(Delmore reenters with the dessert tray as Harry speaks and interrupts him. Again, the music stops when Delmore intrudes.)*

DELMORE. I'm sorry but we're out of strawberry cheesecake. Would you like the plain?

HARRY. *(Enraged.)* Will you leave us alone please?!

DELMORE. I'm just trying to do my job, sir.

HARRY. Well, not now.

DELMORE. Do you or don't you want the cheesecake without the strawberries?

HARRY. I want you to go away. *(Delmore sets down the sherbet, the plain cheesecake and two glasses of tea.)*

DELMORE. Enjoy. *(Delmore steps away from them but doesn't exit. He stands at his station folding napkins and shining silverware.)*

HARRY. *(To Rose.)* My God, some nerve …

ROSE. *(Anxiously.)* Harry, finish what you were saying …

HARRY. *(Loud enough for Delmore to hear.)* I should report him to the head waiter …

ROSE. Harry, please … finish …

HARRY. *(A beat.)* What I'm saying is … *(The music begins to build again as he speaks.)* I can promise you a comfortable life, Rose. You'll never have to worry about anything. I'll take care of you always, Rose, I'll make sure your pretty face stays smiling always.

ROSE. You think I'm pretty, Harry?

HARRY. Yes. Very pretty.

ROSE. *(Softly, pleased.)* Oh. Good.

HARRY. And, Rose, I'll be good to you. You'll never be cold or hungry. I'll give you anything you want.

ROSE. Children, Harry? *(Delmore drops some silverware and bends down to pick them up.)*

HARRY. *(Glances at Delmore; a beat.)* If that's what you want … *(Rose nods.)* So then, Rose … *(Nervously.)* What do you think? *(He sighs.)* Will you be my wife? *(Delmore stands over the fallen silver-ware, frozen and helpless as he watches this momentous event. The music continues.)*

ROSE. *(Welling up with tears.)* Yes! Yes. Harry, I will! It would make me so happy to be your wife!

DELMORE. *(With dread, to himself.)* Oh, no …

ROSE. *(Excited, tearful.)* I had a feeling you were going to ask me today.

HARRY. You did?

ROSE. I was *hoping* you would, from the first time I saw you. "What a respectable gentleman," I thought to myself.

DELMORE. *(Mounting dread and panic.)* Oh, no …

HARRY. *(Also laughing, caught up in the moment.)* Oh yes? Well, I always knew you were a girl with good judgment. *(Rose and Harry laugh, Rose through her tears.)* So, it's a deal, then?

ROSE. Oh, yes, Harry, it's a deal. *(Harry picks up his glass of tea, Rose hers. They prepare for a toast. Refers to glass.)* Oooh, it's hot …

HARRY. To us! …

ROSE. … And our exceptional future! *(They're about ready to drink when Delmore exclaims:)*

DELMORE. DON'T! *(Rose and Harry stop. They look at him. The music also stops.)* Don't do it!

ROSE. Harry, what is he carrying on?

DELMORE. *(Distraught.)* It's not too late to change your minds, both of you. There's still time …

HARRY. What are you getting so excited about?

DELMORE. *(A beat.)* Your desserts … you can still change your orders! You can still have the chocolate layer cake! It's not too late!

HARRY. *(To Rose.)* Don't pay any attention to him.

DELMORE. Please … there's still time …

ROSE. What's wrong with him?

HARRY. Crazy waiter.

DELMORE. Please …

HARRY. Ignore him. *(Harry raises his glass. Rose with an eye still on Delmore, lifts hers.)* To us.

ROSE. To us. *(They touch glasses.)*

DELMORE. *(Covers his eyes with his hands.)* Oh, no … *(Tableau: Rose and Harry in the middle of their toast. Rose is looking at Delmore, whose face is in his hands. Lights begin to fade except for the spots on their faces. Fade out. The sound of the ocean is heard in the darkness.)*

SCENE SIX

A photographer's booth on the boardwalk. Rose and Harry are posed before a camera on a tripod. Delmore, as the photographer, is hidden beneath the black drape of the camera. Delmore steps out from under the drape and assesses the pose. He goes to Harry and arranges his hand on Rose's shoulder. Rose giggles. Delmore carefully looks over the pose then thinks of an addition. He scurries to a corner and gets a bouquet of artificial flowers. Harry rolls his eyes exasperatedly. Delmore arranges the flowers in Rose's arms. Rose giggles. Delmore hurries back under the drape. His hand protrudes clutching the rubber ball. It appears that he's about to take the picture when he decides not to and comes out from under the drape again. Harry sighs impatiently; Rose giggles in an attempt to pacify him. Delmore, meanwhile, is scrutinizing their pose: Something about it isn't right. He thinks of something to correct it and scurries to another corner. He returns with a chair and seats Rose in it. Delmore continually adjusts Rose's position on the chair. His perfectionism annoys Harry; Harry taps his foot in impatience. Delmore finishes arranging Rose and then takes Harry's arm to place it properly. Harry violently yanks his arm from Delmore's hold and glares at him. Delmore returns to the camera and goes beneath the drape. In a beat, he timidly pokes his head out to offer a new adjustment.

HARRY. *(Cutting Delmore off.)* Take the picture, dammit! *(Delmore squeezes the ball. A burst of light; the picture is taken. Tableau: Harry is frozen in an angry grimace, Rose's smile is uncomfortable and overcompensating. Silence. Blackout. The sound of the ocean is heard in the darkness.)*

SCENE SEVEN

A gypsy fortune teller's booth on the boardwalk. Delmore, as the gypsy, is seated by a table on which is a crystal ball. Rose and Harry enter, strolling on the boardwalk.

ROSE. Oooh, Harry, let's get our fortune told!

HARRY. You don't really want to, do you?

ROSE. Yes. It would be fun. Come. We'll see what the future holds.

HARRY. Why would you want to do that?

ROSE. Aren't you even a little bit curious?

HARRY. No.

ROSE. Come on, Harry ... Please ...

HARRY. This is nonsense, Rose.

ROSE. It's only twenty-five cents.

HARRY. Twenty-five cents too much.

DELMORE. Fortune?

HARRY. Let's go.

ROSE. *(Petulantly.)* No.

HARRY. All they do is make up lies and deceive people.

ROSE. I'm going in. Are you coming with me? *(Pause. Harry begrudgingly follows her to the booth.)*

DELMORE. Twenty-five cents. *(Rose looks to Harry; he fishes in his pocket for a quarter and hands it to Delmore. Delmore looks the coin over suspiciously, then pockets it. To Rose.) Sit. (Rose sits expectantly. Delmore dramatically unveils the crystal ball; Harry rolls his eyes. Delmore moves his hands over the crystal ball, peers into it.)* Hmm ...

ROSE. Gypsy, what do you see?

DELMORE. It doesn't look good ...

HARRY. What nonsense ... *(Rose shushes Harry.)*

DELMORE. Perhaps you don't want me to tell you what I see.

HARRY. You're right.

ROSE. No, tell me.

DELMORE. I see a future filled with remorse, hatred, scandal ...

ROSE. What?

DELMORE. ... lingering bitterness, deceit ...

ROSE. *(Skeptical but good humored.)* That can't be ...

HARRY. Utter nonsense ...

DELMORE. I see a loss of fortune ...

HARRY. Poppycock ...

DELMORE. ... destitution, infidelity, early death ...

HARRY. Rose, it's a racket, come, let's go ...

ROSE. Gypsy, do you have another crystal ball? You're giving someone else's fortune, not ours ...

HARRY. These are nothing but children's toys! Crystal balls! Come, Rose ...

ROSE. Gypsy, look into the ball again. Will we have children?

HARRY. Rose, I can't listen to this ...

DELMORE. Yes, you will have children.

ROSE. Harry, listen ...

DELMORE. A son ...

ROSE. Harry, a son!

DELMORE. A son whose character will be monstrous.

ROSE. No, that can't be ...

HARRY. Rose, I can't stand this anymore ... *(Harry tugs Rose's arm and tries to pull her to her feet, she resists.)*

DELMORE. *(To Harry.)* What's the matter? Can't you bear the truth?

HARRY. Truth?! This isn't truth, this is a terrible joke! You shouldn't be allowed to do this, you should be run off the boardwalk! Rose ...

ROSE. I want the gypsy to look into another ball ...

HARRY. Well, very well then, Rose, you do whatever you want ... *(Harry angrily strides out of the booth and off the stage.)*

ROSE. *(Choking back tears; a shriek.)* Harry! Harry, wait! *(Rose starts to run after Harry, but Delmore takes hold of her arm. Rose tries to break the hold but cannot. She looks at Delmore in confusion.)*

DELMORE. Don't. *(Pause. Rose considers Delmore's request.)*

ROSE. Let go of my arm!

DELMORE. Don't go after him.

ROSE. I have to! What will I do if I don't go after him? Huh? Let go of me, I have to catch up with him! *(Pause. Delmore considers*

Rose's remark, then lets her go.) Harry, wait! I'm coming! *(Rose runs off, taking a final glimpse of Delmore before she exits. Delmore is alone. As the lights begin to fade, he takes off his costume, revealing the pajamas he wore in the first scene. He stands with his back to the audience. Fade out. The sound of a movie projector is heard in the darkness.)*

SCENE EIGHT

As in Scene One, the stage is empty except for a movie theatre seat in which Delmore sits facing the audience. There's an over-turned box of popcorn at his feet. Tears stream down his cheeks. A light flickers on the audience from behind Delmore. We hear a crescendo of romantic music, signifying the end of the "movie." In a beat, lights come full up. The Usher (played by the elder Rose, dressed as she was in Scene One) enters with a broom and dust pan and begins sweeping up the aisles of the theatre.

USHER. A real tearjerker, huh? Don't you love the way she runs back to him at the end? I love happy endings.
DELMORE. You think that was a happy ending?
USHER. Sure, they both got what they wanted, didn't they.
DELMORE. Yes …
USHER. I mean, *he* wanted *her* and you could tell by the way she looked at him she was crazy about the guy. You've got to admit, the guy had a certain charm.
DELMORE. It had to be that way.
USHER. Yeah.
DELMORE. It *had* to be that way. It was fate.
USHER. Fate? Yeah, fate. Hand me that box of popcorn. *(He does.)* Now, you better clear out of here …
DELMORE. Can't I stay for a little while longer?
USHER. No. I've got to close the place up.
DELMORE. Do you mind if I stay a little longer?
USHER. Yes, I mind.

45

DELMORE. It's very comfortable here.

USHER. I'm glad you like it but you can't stay.

DELMORE. Please, just a little longer.

USHER. Young man, you're being a nuisance.

DELMORE. I'll help you sweep up.

USHER. Look, it's time, do I have to throw you out myself?

DELMORE. I want to stay.

USHER. Well, you *can't* stay! You can't do whatever you want in this world, young man ... *(She pulls him out of the seat and begins to push him out.)* Now, go, get out of here ... Go! *(She pokes him with the broom; Delmore exits. She looks off at him and shakes her head. Fade out. Amplified sound of phonograph needle skipping on a record, as in the Prologue.)*

EPILOGUE

December 1934. The kitchen of the Schwartz apartment, the morning following the Prologue. The skipping phonograph needle fades into the sound of a barely audible radio. Rose sets two glasses with tea bags on the kitchen table. She carefully arranges the morning newspaper at one of the place settings. She warms her hands over a tea kettle on the stove then sits and looks out the window. In a beat, Delmore enters; he's still wearing his pajamas. Rose senses his presence, turns to look at him, smiles, returns to the window. Silence.

ROSE. It snowed.

DELMORE. A lot?

ROSE. Enough. *(Pause.)* I thought I'd let you sleep on account it's your birthday.

DELMORE. Thanks. *(Pause.)* Good morning.

ROSE. Good morning. How does it feel to be twenty-one?

DELMORE. Cold.

ROSE. Put on some clothes you won't be cold. I put up some water for tea.

DELMORE. Good. *(Pause.)*

ROSE. The morning paper's here.

DELMORE. I see.

ROSE. I went out and got the paper.

DELMORE. In the snow?

ROSE. In the snow. So what. It's your birthday, I figured you'd like to read the paper when you got up.

DELMORE. Thank you.

ROSE. Happy birthday.

DELMORE. Thanks.

ROSE. Twenty-one.

DELMORE. Yes. *(Pause.)*

ROSE. So, are you glad to have the paper?

DELMORE. Very, yes.

ROSE. Good. *(Pause.)*

DELMORE. Ma, I had a dream.

ROSE. A good dream? A bad dream?

DELMORE. I think I cried in my sleep.

ROSE. What did you dream that made you cry? *(Pause. Delmore considers describing the dream to her but decides not to.)*

DELMORE. I can't remember.

ROSE. If you can't remember, chances are it wasn't important. *(A beat.)*

DELMORE. Ma, would you do something for me?

ROSE. *(Unsure.)* Do something? What? *(Delmore exits the kitchen. Calls after him.)* Where you going?! I put up water! *(In a beat, Delmore returns carrying Rose's sewing basket; he extends it to her. At first she doesn't know why he's handing it to her, then recalls the discussion of her ripped sweater. Rose thinks it over, then takes the basket from him. Delmore sits at the table. Rose takes off her sweater and joins him there. Soon Delmore becomes involved in reading the newspaper while Rose threads a needle and begins to mend her sweater. The tea kettle whistles. Fade out.)*

End of Play

MISADVENTURE

MISADVENTURE premiered at the Humana Festival of New American Plays at Actors Theatre of Louisville (Jon Jory, Producing Director) in Louisville, Kentucky, in March 2000 as a part of the "dramatic anthology" *Back Story*, based on characters created by Joan Ackermann. It was directed by Meredith McDonough; the set design was by Paul Owen; the lighting design was by Greg Sullivan; the sound design was by Martin R. Desjardins; the costume design was by Kevin McLeod; the dramaturgs were Amy Wegener and Michael Bigelow Dixon; and the stage manager was Amber D. Martin. Ainsley was played by Kimberly Megna and Ethan was played by Cary Calebs.

MISADVENTURE

The parking lot of the Danville, New Hampshire, police station. Ainsley, twenty-one, is fuming. Ethan, seventeen, is hungover and sheepish. It's cold.

AINSLEY. Get in the car.
ETHAN. *(Refusing.)* Un-uh.
AINSLEY. Get. In. The. Car.
ETHAN. No way.
AINSLEY. Ethan! Get in the car!
ETHAN. I refuse to get in the car when you're like this.
AINSLEY. Like what?
ETHAN. You're mad at me.
AINSLEY. I am not mad at you.
ETHAN. Yes you are; I can tell: Your nostrils are doing that thing.
AINSLEY. What thing?
ETHAN. You know, they kinda … *(Demonstrates by flaring his nostrils.)*
AINSLEY. GETINTHECAR!
ETHAN. I'm not getting in any car with you at the wheel when you're like this. What if you lose control and crash into a tree or something?
AINSLEY. I'm not gonna lose control.
ETHAN. How do you know? You might get this uncontrollable urge to smack me repeatedly and then what?
AINSLEY. I am not gonna smack you! Get in the car!
ETHAN. I've had enough trauma for one evening, thank you.
AINSLEY. *You've* had enough trauma!
ETHAN. Yes! The stigma of incarceration will haunt me for years.
AINSLEY. *(Softly.)* Get in the car. *(He shakes his head no.)* Ethan, I am too tired and too pissed-off —

ETHAN. Ah-ha! *(Because she let her anger slip.)*

AINSLEY. *(Continuous.)* — to be having this argument with you in a police station parking lot in Nowhere, New Hampshire, in the middle of a freezing night. I'm cold and I want to go home.

ETHAN. I like the cold; the cold feels good. It's sobering me up. I feel more awake than I've ever felt in my life.

AINSLEY. What were you thinking?! What in the world were you thinking?!

ETHAN. I don't know.

AINSLEY. You don't *know*? Were you trying to *kill* yourself? Huh? *Were* you? *(He shrugs.)* Were you looking to get yourself *killed?*

ETHAN. No. I don't know. Maybe.

AINSLEY. Maybe?! MAYBE?!

ETHAN. I don't know, I said.

AINSLEY. You selfish boy! You stupid selfish boy!

ETHAN. Good. Let it out. I'm glad we're talking now; it's much better than that nostril thing.

AINSLEY. How DARE you be reckless with your life! How DARE you!

ETHAN. Shhh! You're disturbing the peace. You want them to throw both of us in jail?

AINSLEY. What's my life worth if you trash yours? Huh? Have you thought about that?! I'll have to live the next seventy-five years haunted every goddamn day by your pimply ghostly self! We're not just sibs, you stupid moron, we're soulmates! Don't you know that by now?!

ETHAN. *(Childlike, surprised by the depth of her rage, he nods; a beat, then softly.)* I'm sorry.

AINSLEY. You drink yourself sick and go hitching on the interstate?! Are you crazy?! Have I taught you nothing?!

ETHAN. Hey. A. I said I was sorry.

AINSLEY. Never mind being drunk and weaving on the shoulder with cars and trucks whizzing by at eighty miles an hour. Never mind that. What if a crazy person stopped to pick you up — a Jeffrey Dahmer-type or something —

ETHAN. *(Amused.)* What?!

AINSLEY. — and took you away so you were never heard from again! Some Boy Scouts would come across your jawbone one day in the woods. It's a good thing the cops picked you up and threw you in jail. You could've been roadkill.

ETHAN. You're nuts, you know that? You've been watching too much television!

AINSLEY. Don't mock me. There ARE crazy people out there, you know, they're not just CREATED by the media. They exist! There are truly bad and sick people out there in the world who want nothing more than to destroy other people's happiness. *(He cracks up.)* Stop laughing! STOP IT! It isn't funny! You scared me, Ethan! You scared me to death! *(She throws punches at him, he protects his head with his hands, laughing until she really hurts him.)*

ETHAN. Oww! *(She stops. Silence.)* That hurt.

AINSLEY. Good.

ETHAN. I can explain.

AINSLEY. Nothing you could possibly say ...

ETHAN. Aren't you even gonna give me my due process? Aren't you?

AINSLEY. I don't see why I should.

ETHAN. I'm just a kid you know.

AINSLEY. Oh God. Is that your excuse? Is that your pissant excuse?!

ETHAN. Kids are *supposed* to act out and do reckless things. Right? If not while I'm young, when? When I'm old? When I'm forty?

AINSLEY. The key is surviving long enough to attain wisdom.

ETHAN. Okay, so I survived.

AINSLEY. You're not a cat, though, Ethan; that's what worries me: You only get one shot and you came awfully close this time ...

ETHAN. Okay, so let's chalk it up to the folly of youth. Okay? I've learned my lesson: I drank a whole lot of really shitty bourbon with some asshole I don't even like whose approval I inexplicably crave and blew Pizza Hut pizza all down my front and onto my brand new running shoes. Don't you think I'm humiliated enough? I just *bought* these shoes. Like a week ago.

AINSLEY. If you'd killed yourself! ... If you'd gotten yourself killed for some stupid, peer-pressure, macho, adolescent, alcoholic misadventure ... If I'd lost you 'cause of it ... If I'd *lost* you ... *(She finally lets herself weep; she turns away from him. He's impressed. Silence.)* Pizza Hut, huh. No wonder you smell like a dairy farmer.

ETHAN. I can't even smell it anymore.

AINSLEY. Trust me.

ETHAN. Oh, yeah, why should I trust you?

AINSLEY. Because you'd better. Because if you don't trust me, brother, you are a goner. You are toast. *(A beat.)* Now get in the car.

ETHAN. Still mad at me?

AINSLEY. *(Smiling.)* Get in the fucking car?

ETHAN. *(Smiles; a beat; as he gets into the car.)* Can we stop somewhere to get something to eat? I'm starving.

AINSLEY. We'll see. Phew. You stink. *(She starts the car.)*

End of Play

LOUIE

LOUIE, ANTHONY, JOEY and LOLA were first presented as part of *Tuna on Rye and Other Short Pieces* in New York's Ensemble Studio Theater's 1983 Octoberfest. The plays were directed by Willie Reale and performed by Larry Block (Louie), Millard Corbett (Anthony), Keith Gordon (Joey) and Marcia Haufrecht (Lola).

LOUIE

An older, hearing-impaired man.

LOUIE. I know how long ago it happened 'cause of that picture? *From Here to Eternity?* When Pearl Harbor. Round there. Pearl Harbor, there in Hawaii. *(Pause.)* I was gonna enlist. In the navy? Came out 4-F. They called me back a year later anyways, guess to make sure I was still 4-F. *(Pause.)* I think it happened 'cause once on 34th Street?, they were digging up the street. And I was crossing, waiting for the light. And I was standing right next to one of those guys with the big noisy — *(Uses his hands to show a jackhammer.)* Y'know what I mean? Prolly not, though, right? Nah. Prolly not. *(Pause.)* Threw me outta school 'cause of it. Least if I'd've been nineteen, least I'd've had a diploma from high school, least I'd've got a real job, maybe. They dint wanna give what you call special attention. Nowadays it's different. I wanna go back to school. I see in the paper they got this city college gives special attention for deaf people. You think they would take me? Huh? I got partial hearing. I can still hear a little with a hearing aid. Like I could hear the lady next door sometimes. She yells, I hear her. *(Pause.)* Like you, you speak clear so I can talk to you. Some people, they turn their heads, they expect me to hear! I say, "'Scuse me," or "Par'n me." They're so dumb. The lipreading teacher said the best thing is to talk to people who hear normal. Even five minutes at a time. It's very important, she says. She got married. Then she left again to have kids. You can't talk to everybody, though, 'cause not everybody speaks clear. *Five* minutes, even. *(Holds his outstretched palms up; pause.)* You can go a little nuts with so much no sound. Sometimes I turn it to Channel 13. Opera I can hear. Beverly Sills? Her I can hear. I can hear some of her sounds. Sometimes I can follow what's on the TV but I keep the voice part down. All that noise! I have to put the voice part all the way up to hear just a little bit so it's not worth all the noise. And the lady next door, she yells. *(Pause.)* Take Crosby. I can't hear. Bing Crosby, he sings too low for me. Perry Como? Him, too. I can hear him singing, but I can't *hear* him. *(Pause.)* Does that make sense? Sometimes I catch maybe it'll be a couple words. Y'know what that's like? Like tasting ice cream, you wanna hear more. *(Pause.)* I wanna learn to take pictures. Photographer. *(Pause.)* You think they'd give a driver's license to a deaf person? Prolly not. What if I put on big rearview mirrors? On both sides. Twice the size of regular ones. *(Pause.)* The blind got it better. Yeah, they're better off. Least they can talk. Least they can put on a record.

End of Play

ANTHONY

ANTHONY

A twelve-year-old boy.

ANTHONY. They called the cops. You should have been there. Flashing lights and everything. And the honking, and all the bright headlights, and the kids and everybody in the street: "Jump! Jump!" Everybody was out of their house. There was a big crowd. My father, he let me get up on his shoulders so I saw everything great. I was the highest kid there and I could see everything. I saw the hair of everybody in the crowd. And my little brother, Edward, he cried because he wanted to see, too, but my father wouldn't let him, he only let me. Because I'm older, and also because when he saw what was really going on, he said to my mother, "Irene, take Eddie upstairs, go on." Harlene's mother was on the roof and she was screaming. She took her shirt off so all you saw was her white skin and black bra. She was screaming and she was crying but she was too far up to hear and everybody was talking so loud until she screamed, "Tommy!" Everybody got quiet. "Tommy! Tommy!" She was screaming. Tommy's the super.

Then Tommy got up there on the roof and you could see him by his T-shirt sometimes because it looked white. He was talking but you couldn't hear him. She yelled and called him bad names. He said something else, also, you couldn't hear what. She like walked to the edge of the roof, you could see her standing there. She yelled, "I'm gonna jump, don't go near me!" Everybody got real quiet listening. Then, her shirt fell off the roof. Everybody went: "Oh," all at the same time and some of the older kids climbed the fence and took it out of the tree like they were at a ball game. Harlene's mother looked down at us and everybody looked up and it got quiet again and Billy laughed.

And then you saw it: A cop came out of the dark on the roof

and grabbed Harlene's mother and pulled her back into the dark and you couldn't see her anymore. Some of the older kids went: "Boo!" and some of the grown-ups got angry and some of them clapped. Everybody started to go home. My father bent down to get me off his shoulders. He told me I was breaking his back.

End of Play

JOEY

JOEY

A man in his early twenties.

JOEY. They gave it, it was this big, I'm telling you. Juiciest spare ribs you ever saw and special fried rice we ordered. This big. No shit, big as this. They throw everything in it, big chunks of *pork* they throw in, egg, whatayacallem, *peas* … Vinnie, he wolfs down an egg roll like he's Linda Lovelace or something. You should see him. Duck sauce all over his chin. Fucking pig. There was lots and lots of food. Kept on ordering and ordering like there's no tomorrow. What the fuck did I care? I wasn't laying out for it, shit, it was my fucking birthday. Bill came to like fifty bucks or something, I don't know, sixty maybe. But, oh man, this Wing's Palace, they got like the best fucking egg foo yong you will ever eat in your entire life, I mean if you like egg foo yong. And Douglas? He got like the number six whatayacallem? combo jobs? Wing's Palace special chow mein. They throw *lob*ster in it, *spare* ribs, *pork* they got, uh, *shrimp*, *spare* ribs, you name it it's in there. We was all like sharing food, me, Vinnie, William, and this faggot Douglas was guarding his plate like it was Fort Knox or something. We was all like eating off each other's plate, you know tasting here and there?, except for Douglas who, I'm telling you, is acting like a faggot. Everybody else is like sharing, having a good time, swigging the six-pack from under the table, making a mess when you open the can and the beer sprays the old couple at the next booth, and the Chink he's getting like real upset, his fucking floor is sticky from beer, I mean it's really worth it to have a heart attack over spilled beer, right? This is a school night, I might add. And me? Fuck them, I figured why not, I order the most expensive thing on the menu: Wing's Palace Lobster Deluxe. I die from lobster. I figured what the shit, I'm the birthday boy, I deserve it. Shit, I'm like a father to these

65

boys. I mean, it is *real* expensivo but so what? Douglas, naturally, right? Douglas puts up a stink: "Who the fuck you think you are," blah blah blah. I mean, this is an asshole. This is a useless piece of dick. Douglas, with a memory like a retarded elephant, is telling me *who-the-fuck-are-you.* I mean — and this is not a long time ago — Douglas, and I might add, this Douglas is no Robert Redford — Douglas, he's trying so fucking hard it was pathetic to make out with this nothing tease he meets, I don't know, some girl he meets somewheres. When his cousin got married he picked her up at the wedding, something like that. This is out in *Rock*ville he goes, he couldn't find a girl in Sheepshead Bay or something more local, no, he has to go allaway out to fucking Rockville *Cen*tre just to like get his rocks off on this nothing chick, Roberta her name was. You think *I* got bad skin? Man, you should see *her.* Zits like *dimes* man, *this* big, no shit, all over her head. So what happens he goes allaway out to Rockville fucking Centre? Guess. You got it. She don't want to have nothing to do with him if you know what I mean. Is this a nothing tease or what? I advised him on this in the very very beginning. I told him, "Douglas, lay off this Roberta. I know girls like this from personal experience," I told him, "they were put on this earth to turn balls blue, forget her." He don't listen to his friend Joey, naturally, and this Roberta like slaps his hands and says: "Nothing doing, dildo," so Douglas, he's like in this parking lot in this *mall* out in *Rock*ville with blue marbles in his pants, a tease in the front seat won't have nothing to do with him, and his fucking car like *dies* on him. Cardiac arrest, man. Poof! The thing won't fart to save his life. So what does he do? He calls me up fucking collect from this pay phone in this shopping mall in Rockville Centre, Long Island. And me! I accept the charge like an asshole. And he don't *ask:* "Can you do me a favor and so and so," no, the prick *tells* me: "Joey you gotta come get me." I *gotta.* Do you believe this? It's fucking one A.M. My old lady got real pissed and I don't blame her, I mean who likes getting a call from an asshole at one o'clock in the morning? And William was over the house. We was getting stoned on the porch whenever there was a commercial. *Saturday Night Live* is really beginning to suck. So, anyway, like a total asshole, I don't say: "Douglas, fuck off," no, so me and William, who is even more wrecked than me, me and William we get into my car — do not ask me why I do this please — and we take this ride out to this fucking stupid absolute dildo in a dead car in a parking lot in Rockville fucking Centre, Long Island. And I'm driving there and driving there and I am seeing triple and I'm screaming at William: "What the sign say? Tell me what the sign say," and he keeps saying: "Slow down, Joe, I can't read them." I'm telling you, this is what I have to put up with. Finally, I mean after all this, we find the stupid fucking shopping mall and there's Douglas, sleeping on the steering wheel like a drunk driver or something. Girl skipped out on him, poor prick. So what do I do? Jump his car, straighten him out, give him a little pep talk (you know, like don't take it so hard, she was a nothing tease from the word go). I follow right behind him on the highway, make sure he don't decide to jump lanes and kill himself or anything, take him home to his mother and practically tuck him in. Did this fucking asshole ever once say to me: "Thanks a lot, Joey," or "Joe, what a friend." Huh? *(Pause.)* So what the fuck if I order lobster?

End of Play

LOLA

LOLA

A Polish refugee. Lightly, animatedly.

LOLA. I met my husband Liberation Day. I lost my *sis*ter Liberation Day. I don't know how she dies, but she does. On Liberation Day. A lot of people lost people Liberation Day. The mourning period was very short in those days — if you planned on surviving. No time for shiva. If there was time for shiva, oh God, we all would've died. There was so much of it: death. All over the place. And, my sister, who I'll tell you I happened to love very much, *very* much. I never saw her again. What could I do? By that time, Papa, Mama, my brother Izzy who was never too smart, they were all dead. Not *me,* and there was nothing I could do about it; right? What could I have done, this little pip-squeak? That's what I looked like when my husband met me. I was a real *meiskeit.* You know what that means in Jewish? Uh … uh … what you kids, my daughter, calls a real loser: "Oh, Ma, is that Sharon a real loser." *(A beat.)* I looked a real *meiskeit* because I almost lost my life, that's why. Auschwitz wasn't Grossinger's, honey. Three meals a day? Forget it! Shuffleboard? Go on! You've read about it, I'm sure. Well, it was worse than that, believe me, and I got there like at the tail end. They stopped giving numbers by the time I got there. They must've run out of numbers. Like at the bakery. You notice I don't have numbers on my arm? Well, that's the reason: They ran out of 'em. *(A beat.)* So, I was a *meiskeit.* I wasn't the beauty I am today. I had typhoid. My teeth were falling out. I was very skinny, as you could imagine. Knock-kneed. So, between the teeth missing and my knees knocking, I was not your typical bathing-suit beauty. But my husband, I don't know, somehow he saw something. You see, he comes up to me Liberation Day. Somebody points me out to him: "Go, look, that girl there, she's from Lodz."

71

That's where I lived before the camps. Turns out my husband, he, too, lived in the Lodz ghetto. I didn't know him. But, wait, I'll tell you — he comes up to me, a good-looking guy, not too tall, I look him up and down: Hmm, I think to myself, not bad. He says to me: "Excuse me, I hear you're from the Lodz ghetto." I nodded. I didn't want to keep my mouth open too much, this good-looking guy might see all my teeth that fell out, so I nodded uh-huh. "Tell me," he said, "I'm looking for someone. From Lodz. Can you tell me if you happen to know if she's alive? Her name is Lola. She is a beautiful girl with a magical smile and a sense of humor you could *plotz*. Tell me," he said, "do you know if she survived?" I asked him what street does this Lola live on in the ghetto. He told me. It was my street. And what address? He told me. It was my address. And what was the last name of her family? *(A beat.)* "That's me!" I screamed, all of the spaces in my magical smile showing. "That's me! I am Lola!" And he carried me away, and, like the whole thing was a dream … I woke up: a housewife in Flatbush making gefilte fish for her family. A boy and a girl. Today, that boy has a daughter named for my sister, and the girl, the girl is a clinical psychologist.

End of Play

MANNY

MANNY was commissioned and first presented by The Passage Theatre Company in Trenton, New Jersey, on June 20, 1986. It was directed by Brian Delate and performed by Thomas G. Waites.

MANNY

A twenty-five-year-old man.

MANNY. You just come from the bathroom? You look like a guy just come from the bathroom. You saw what went *on* in there? Oh, these kids, these black kids, took a briefcase. About this big. Brown. Leather, *you* know.

Guy in a business suit, a *lawyer,* sonofabitch is a lawyer I bet. *Looked* like a lawyer. I've seen *lawyers* looked like that. He was drunk. He was drinking. Comes off the train, he can't hold it. I'm standing up taking a leak. Sonofabitch runs in, can't hold it. Drops his briefcase. *Out*side the john, *you* know, with the door? Leaves his thing *out*side and shuts the door! What a jackass thing to do! I see him doing this and I think: This guy is asking for it. A *lawyer.* These guys you expect would know better, but no. So, he's in there farting and belching, trying to get his drunk piss flowing, and these two black kids come in and I think: uh-oh, trouble.

One-two-three, that briefcase is *gone.* Those little pricks are off and running. I knew it. The second they came in. I can tell these things. The sonofabitch comes out wetting himself, fixing his belt, his face pink like a heart attack, and he's screaming: "Hey! I got my money in there!"

What kind of fucking asshole *attorney* does something as stupid as putting his money in a thing and leaving it *out*side the john? No wonder he gets ripped off. What a way to go through life.

This friend of mine? Had this gun. Not me, it was his. I don't have no gun. The service, yeah. The army, yes. I'm talking *civilian* y'understand. Civilian. I don't use guns. I don't *shoot* guns. Oh, yeah, once. Went hunting. Upstate New York. Hunting, like for deers. Wasn't the season, though. Just shot at things. *You* know, like for practice. Target practice. Beer cans and shit.

Aside from that, besides that, I never had a gun on my *person* before. Except for this time with this friend. I got busted. He carries a gun, this friend. Like for protection. I'm not gonna tell you his name 'cause you may know him and I want to respect his privacy.

It's a very small world. You never know. I'm very careful about these things. I don't say names in restaurants 'cause you never know who's sitting behind you. (This is how I go through life.) You may know him and he may not want you knowing this, so don't ask me his name 'cause I ain't telling. His name is irrevelent. [Sic] I'll tell you *my* name. 'Cause I don't care. I'm *talk*ing to you. Got your face memorized. I'll remember you next time I see you. I'm good at that. But *him?*, my friend? Forget it. I ain't telling. Me? I'm Manny. Nice to meet you, too.

So, this is 'round Christmas I'm talking about. My friend, he shows me this gun. Like we were hanging out his place watching wrestling or something? He shows me this gun, right? And I go, "Hey, man, you got a gun? Let's go stick somebody up." I'm kidding, right? And he goes, "You want?" And, like, I'm smiling but I'm not really? You know what I mean? Like I'm thinking: Is he kidding or what? And he goes, "Let's go out." And I go, "It's cold out, man, it's Christmas." He goes, "Exactly." And I think to myself: Shit, this is like two days before Christmas ... I could use some extra bucks. *Pre*sents and stuff. Everybody could use a little extra 'round the holidays. *You* know how it is. My girlfriend just so happened to be pregnant at the time, so, *you* know, I wanted to like give her something to cheer her up. *Christmas* and everything. I mean, there was a certain logic to it. We weren't gonna *hurt* nobody. Just scare. I don't hurt nobody 'less I have to. I don't go out of my way in other words.

So we went out. Not too cold, but cold. I was wearing a, you know, reddish coat, and my friend's gun, it was in my pocket. I loaded it personally. Only two or three bullets in there, tops. Not six. Definitely not six. And we go down to Dwight Street. And we hang out in this lot? Near the pizza place? And we're waiting. And waiting. People go. Couples. Too complicated.

And we wait. And it's getting cold. And then I see this lady coming. Carrying packages. You know: shopping bags. Presents. And I say to Rudy, "Let's go." And we come out of the lot and I go, "Give me your presents and (*you* know) your pocketbook." And she starts giving us a hard time. Says her husband's watching from the window. "Bull*shit.*" "He's watching," she goes. And Rudy goes. (Shit!) My *friend* goes, "Look, lady, we just want your presents and your money. Don't be stupid." And she goes, "I will not! Blah-blah-blah-blah-blah!" And she's yelling and I'm thinking: shit. And he goes, "Lady, shut up or we're gonna shoot you." And she yells. And I think: What if a police car comes? I mean, they *do.* A police car *is* gonna come by sooner or later. I *am* a logical person. So I go to my friend, I go, "Let's quit this shit." And I tell the lady, "Listen, I won't kill you this time. But just don't call the cops, okay?" And she goes, "Yes, yes, of course." And we go. And I say to her, "Merry Christmas, lady."

Cops picked us up two blocks later. Bitch went ahead and told them. She tells! I spared her life and she tells! I wished her a Happy New Year and everything! Shit.

Got off easy. Dumped the gun. But still … What a way to go through life. Can't trust nobody. Got to look out every second.

I been a victim. I know about these things. I was mugged myself. I was opening up my car. Two guys come up to me like out of nowheres. White guys. They got a knife. You see this scar? Cut my whole face open. Like you could peel my whole skin off. Cut me deep. The blood was amazing. I chased *after* the scumbag. Other guy got away. I went after the scumbag who cut me.

Never run away from them.
Make them run away from you.

I caught up with this guy. I couldn't see 'cause of the blood, but I grabbed him and knocked him down on the ground. And I whipped out this hammer, see. I had this hammer on me. I whipped out this hammer and bam! bam! Hit him in the head. Bam! Bam! More and more and more. Couldn't stop. Like it was uncontrollable. I had no control over it. Bam! Bam! Bam! Till his head, you could stuff tomatoes in it.

Self-defense. I got off. Fucking lawyer almost did me in, the sonofabitch. Lawyers.

What a way to go through life.

End of Play

I DON'T KNOW
WHAT I'M DOING

For Didi Conn

I DON'T KNOW WHAT I'M DOING

A woman in her thirties.

NANCY. Excuse me, I don't know what I'm doing. I bought a one-way ticket for Madison. I've never been to Wisconsin. I know one person in the whole state. Is it cold this time of year? I didn't think. I got on the plane with an overnight bag. Just my toothbrush and a change of undies, practically. I don't know what I'm doing; I can't believe I'm doing this. *(A beat.)* I'm going to see an old friend. For a visit. But it's sort of a surprise. I mean it *is* a surprise because he doesn't know I'm coming. I hope he's there; I've got an address. *(Takes out an envelope with letter.)* True, the letter's from 1979, but I'm hoping he didn't move around much. How big can Madison *be?* (A beat.) This was the letter I got from him, congratulating me on my wedding. He said that by the time his mother forwarded the invitation to him it was too late for him to come but that that was alright 'cause he didn't think he would've come anyway. *(Reads from letter.)* "If you picked Steve out of all the guys in the world, he must be one terrific guy." Ha. "Have a good life, Nancy. Be fruitful, etcetera. Remember me always and I'll do the same for you. Billy. P.S. Save me a piece of wedding cake." *(Puts letter back in envelope.)*

Billy and I used to play married. In high school, we'd cut out and go to his house after his mother went to work and take off our clothes and get under the covers of his parents' double bed and roll around each other. We never did it; he never tried; I took that as a sign of how much he loved me. But I'd lie on top of him, naked, and we'd talk about everything, *every*thing — school, friends, Janis Joplin, mothers and fathers — and whisper and laugh, and feel

83

our breaths get hot, and we'd lie like that for hours, till we were tired and sweaty, and then we'd take a shower together. We'd do that all the time it seemed, but maybe it was just a couple of times. I would hang out in front of school and wait for him, right before I'd have to go into homeroom, wait for him with my heart pounding in my ears, hoping he'd show up and take me back to his parents' bed and take off my clothes and talk to me. He talked to me like nobody else. Like nobody else before or since. The sound of his voice wrapped me up like a blanket. I could lay in his voice forever, soft and warm, his breath on me.

(A beat.)

He had the littlest tush, Billy; his pants would hang in the back where his tush should be. And his eyes were small and brown but they always *looked* at you. Some people even with big eyes don't, they don't really *look* at you. I made him laugh. He told me I was beautiful.

(A beat.)

We slept on the beach one night before we graduated, Brighton Beach. Under the boardwalk where the sand was cold and didn't smell like sand. You could see the moonlight through the slats on the sand. You could hear somewhere out in the dark some kids going at it, and the ocean, and sometimes people walking up above and the wood creaking. And I lay on top of Billy, with our clothes on, and whispered and laughed till we both fell asleep, tired from all that wonderful talk. I woke up at that strange hour when the sky isn't quite morning yet, and you happen to be up when the streetlights click off? We didn't plan to fall asleep, it just happened. When I got home it was around 5:30 and my father was sitting in his chair in his underwear smoking a cigarette and my mother was snoring on the sofa. My father was so mad at me he didn't even yell. He cried. He sobbed. "How could you do this?" he said, over and over. "Nancy, Nancy, Nancy. How could you do this?" And I said, "I don't know what I'm doing." I wanted to tell him we were talking, me and Billy, we were only talking, but instead I told him I didn't know what I was doing.

(A beat.)

My father made it very hard for me to see Billy again after that. We graduated and I went to Brooklyn College and he went upstate, to Binghamton. The next time I saw him was Thanksgiving of our freshman year when he came home. I was with my family and he was with his, and we were going into a Chinese restaurant on Ocean Avenue and they were just leaving. We were like Romeo and Juliet, our parents muttering hellos and looking at each other funny as we walked past like the enemy. I thought I would die, that my heart would stop pumping and I would collapse and die. That night I called him and snuck out of the house and met him at the boardwalk. I didn't care what would happen, I had to see him. He was stoned when he got there, and his little eyes were puffy and bloodshot, and his beautiful voice was hoarse from all that smoke. He didn't sound like Billy anymore. We went under the boardwalk. I had so much to tell him, so much to talk to him about. It was November and freezing, not like it was in May, and he got on top of *me* this time. This time he didn't want to talk.

(Pause.)

I can't blame him. It was my fault he was the way he was. If I'd stood up to my father and told him nothing happened that night, if I'd only told him all we did was talk, I would've still been allowed to see Billy and he wouldn't've gotten stoned, and the thing that happened that night wouldn't've happened. I ran home hysterical. My father heard my crying and knocked on my door and asked, very nicely really, if I was okay; he asked like he knew what happened, but I wanted to tell him all about it anyway but I didn't and he went back to bed.

(Pause.)

This tall, skinny, sort of cute boy in my Intro to Drama class, who had been asking me out every couple of weeks and I kept putting him off and putting him off, well, he asked me again the Monday after Thanksgiving if I would go out with him and I said yes. He had big green eyes and his name was Steve and four years later I married him.

(Pause; she takes a wedge of something wrapped in tinfoil out of her bag.)

Nine-year-old wedding cake. I kept it in my freezer, moved five times with it packed in dry ice. It can't taste like much, but that's not the point. Billy asked me to save him a piece. *(Pause; her eyes suddenly fill with tears, she smiles brightly and blushes.)* I still love him. *(She shrugs.)*

End of Play

SOMNAMBULIST

SOMNAMBULIST

WOMAN. I saw my feet. I was lying on my back. My head was even propped up with pillows. I had just set the book I was reading face down on the floor. The last words I read were ... "We begin to find ... " Then I began to doze. It was an innocuous drifting; I had no idea that I was about to doze away and not merely to sleep. As I said, I set the book down. It didn't fall from my hands as you later speculated. I put it there; it may have gotten kicked or tossed in the confusion, but I was the one who had placed it there. *(Pause.)* Then ... I slept for a few seconds which seemed like much longer. It was the kind of distracted, momentary dozing you do while riding the subway. Rush hour drifting. Your head rolls and falls, waking you, and then you roll off again. Time becomes segmented by uneasy sleep and the stops along the line on the way home. It was that kind of deceptive dozing; a few seconds which felt like hours.

Suddenly — I'll use that word for want of a better one — for it was sudden, like a light bulb flaring and burning out without warning. Suddenly, I felt a bubble rise in my gut. I tried belching it out because it seemed that easy. I was drowning. I saw my toes twitch. I saw a piece of my underwear sticking out of a drawer. I saw the doorknob and a metal hanger hanging from it. I remembered that the book I was reading was two days overdue at the public library. And then I died.

End of Play

FATHER AND SON

FATHER AND SON

Father (fifties) and Son (twenties) seated at a table in an apartment, looking over a checkbook and check ledger.

FATHER. And what do I put here?

SON. The amount.

FATHER. I get it.

SON. You put in the amount, then you subtract it from the balance.

FATHER. Which is the balance?

SON. The balance. The total you start out with.

FATHER. I get it. So the amount goes here.

SON. Right.

FATHER. And then I subtract the amount from the balance.

SON. Right.

FATHER. So let's say I'm paying Con Ed. Here I write "Con Ed" and where it says amount, I put in how much the check is for.

SON. Right.

FATHER. And then I subtract the amount from the balance. How'm I doing?

SON. Great.

FATHER. This isn't so hard. All those years I thought your mother was doing something so hard and mysterious. This isn't bad at all. I'm doing okay, right?

SON. You're doing great.

FATHER. I'm not such a bad student, am I?

SON. No, it's just that I'm such a good teacher.

FATHER. *(Laughs.)* So anyway, what do I do after I subtract?

SON. Nothing.

FATHER. So what's this number here?

SON. Your new balance.

FATHER. Oh. And then what do I do? I go on to the next check?

SON. Right. And you just do the same thing for each check.

FATHER. I get it. So let's say I write a check out to the phone company.

SON. It's the same procedure.

FATHER. I write in the amount, subtract it, and then I wind up with … I forgot what you called it.

SON. The new balance.

FATHER. Right. And that's all there is to it. That's how you balance a checkbook. Gee.

SON. Well, I gotta go.

FATHER. What time is it?

SON. It's almost seven.

FATHER. Gee, I had no idea.

SON. I don't want to get home too late. The trains are crazy.

FATHER. No, of course not. It'll probably be dark by the time you get home.

SON. Yeah, I know.

FATHER. Well, let me just ask you something.

SON. What?

FATHER. What if I want to write *you* a check?

SON. What do you mean?

FATHER. Do I have to write your whole name in here? *(Meaning the ledger.)*

SON. No.

FATHER. I don't?

SON. No. Nobody's gonna be looking at the book but you.

FATHER. So if I wrote you a check, all I really have to write in here is "Mickey," right? I don't have to write Michael Weiss or anything.

SON. No.

FATHER. I see. I can just write "Mickey" and that'll do.

SON. Dad, I really should go.

FATHER. Of course.

SON. *(Kisses him.)* Take it easy.

FATHER. Naturally. How'm I doing?

SON. You're doing great.

FATHER. Hey, how's your girlfriend?

SON. Fine.

FATHER. She gets more beautiful every time I see her.

94

SON. Yeah … well, I'll speak to you soon.

FATHER. You gonna get the train right here?

SON. Yup.

FATHER. And that'll take you straight to your house?

SON. Uh, yeah, then I walk two blocks.

FATHER. Uh-huh. Okay.

SON. So, you can call me, too, you know.

FATHER. I will …

SON. *(Kisses him.)* So take it easy.

FATHER. Hey, Mick?

SON. What?

FATHER. Come on, I'll take you home. *(Stands.)*

SON. No.

FATHER. I don't want you on the trains. You could get killed.

SON. I ride the trains all the time, don't worry about it.

FATHER. Let me just get my stuff, go to the john …

SON. Forget about it. *60 Minutes* is almost on.

FATHER. So what, I can live without Mike Wallace.

SON. But you love *60 Minutes*.

FATHER. Ah, it's stupid lately. Let me pee.

SON. No, Dad, I'm going.

FATHER. What're you gonna do, such a long train ride.

SON. I've got the puzzle, I'll be fine.

FATHER. The crossword? Your mother was crazy about crosswords. She'd know all the answers one-two-three. *(Pause.)*

SON. Look, this is really silly, Dad, what are you gonna start shlepping to the city for?, you've got a great spot.

FATHER. *(A beat.)* Are you sure?

SON. Yes.

FATHER. Go already, then. I'd have to stop for gas anyway, so go.

SON. Yeah.

FATHER. You better get going.

SON. So long. *(Kisses him, they hug.)*

FATHER. Your mother would have loved your haircut.

End of Play

DEATH IN THE FAMILY

DEATH IN THE FAMILY

A telephone conversation. Mickey is in his twenties; Irving is in his fifties.

MICKEY. Hello?

IRVING. Mickey, this is your Unc.

MICKEY. Hello.

IRVING. How are ya?

MICKEY. How are *you?*

IRVING. Listen: There was a death in the family.

MICKEY. Who?

IRVING. Sidney Grund.

MICKEY. Who's Sidney Grund?

IRVING. I don't know, a cousin of mine and your father's.

MICKEY. You're sure?

IRVING. Yeah, I think so. Listen: I'm calling you to tell your father, so, you tell him a cousin of his died. The funeral's tomorrow, 12:30, Parkside Chapel. You writing this down?

MICKEY. No.

IRVING. Tomorrow, 12:30, Parkside. Write it down.

MICKEY. Are you going?

IRVING. Nah. I don't even know who the guy is. To tell you the honest truth, I don't remember the guy. Jack says he's our cousin, he's our cousin. You have an uncle lives three blocks from you. Talk about families. Jack called me and told me to get in touch with Bob so that's why I called you. Your father gets annoyed — I know this — when nobody tells him when somebody dies. So, tell him: Sidney Grund is being buried tomorrow at Parkside, 12:30. That's the place my wife was buried from. You know, I always said I wanted to be buried standing up, and, you know?, I happen to read this article in the paper: There's a tribe somewheres, they bury their people standing up.

MICKEY. You planning on trying it?

IRVING. Nah. So, how's Bob?

MICKEY. Not so hot.

IRVING. How come?

MICKEY. You know how come.

IRVING. He should get himself a nice girl.

MICKEY. When he's ready.

IRVING. They don't make them like your mother. She was one in a million. He needs a nice girl to listen to him. I know. Me, I look at a girl, she looks at me. She says, Oooh, you're too fat, or too this. Sure I'm fat. Or, I'm too old. Nobody's interested in an old man.

MICKEY. How old are you, Irving?

IRVING. Fifty-eight.

MICKEY. That's very old.

IRVING. Sure it is. They think I'm too old. They don't bother with me, I don't bother with them. What can I tell you? So, you married yet?

MICKEY. No.

IRVING. Why not?

MICKEY. I'm too young for that sort of thing.

IRVING. You've got time.

MICKEY. I hope so.

IRVING. I was married twenty years. It wasn't the greatest. It had its ups and downs. You fight, you make up. It wasn't a bad way to spend twenty years. I don't regret nothing. The first four years, though ... They were the greatest. So, do me a favor, tell your father what I told you. You write it down?

MICKEY. No.

IRVING. What I say?

MICKEY. 12:30, Parkside, tomorrow.

IRVING. You sure you didn't write it down? You got a good memory then. I had to write it down. I don't remember nothing. I'm not a bad guy, I got a bad memory. I'm not a bad guy. Believe me, if I really could've afforded it, I'd've had you over the house. Like the Italians, they're all close and live on top of each other, I would've had you over the house. You make a little more money than a brother, already they're calling you a *goniff*. So just tell your father.

Okay? And tell him his big brother told him he doesn't have to go if he doesn't wanna. 'Bye. Just tell him what I told you. So long.
MICKEY. So long.

End of Play

HOMEWORK

HOMEWORK

Angela, twelve, is doing her homework on her front stoop. Stewie, eighteen, rushes past her.

ANGELA. Hey, Stewie.

STEWIE. Can't talk, Angela.

ANGELA. I need you just a second, Stewie.

STEWIE. What?

ANGELA. Stewie, you know verbs?

STEWIE. Come on, Angela, not now. I gotta go to work.

ANGELA. Stewie I gotta know something about verbs. *(A beat.)*

STEWIE. What about them?

ANGELA. Teach me.

STEWIE. I can't now.

ANGELA. "She is running quickly."

STEWIE. So?

ANGELA. "Is" is the verb?

STEWIE. Yeah.

ANGELA. Right?

STEWIE. Angela, you know this, what do you want from me? *(He starts to walk on.)*

ANGELA. No, wait a minute, Stewie, which one is the proverb?

STEWIE. The what?

ANGELA. The proverb. *(A beat.)*

STEWIE. The proverb?

ANGELA. Yeah. *(Pause.)*

STEWIE. Read over the sentence.

ANGELA. "She is running quickly."

STEWIE. "Quickly." "Quickly" is the proverb.

ANGELA. Yeah?

STEWIE. Yeah. Now, look: I gotta go. I don't got time for you.

ANGELA. Shit, Stewie.

STEWIE. Shut your mouth.

ANGELA. I'm gonna fail.

STEWIE. You're not gonna fail. *(He begins to exit.)*

ANGELA. Motherfucker.

STEWIE. Whoa! What was that?

ANGELA. Nothing.

STEWIE. You better watch it, Angela. I'll tell your brother. He'll beat the shit outta you, tell your mother.

ANGELA. Stewie, just tell me what "running" is.

STEWIE. Look, Angela, this is it: "Running" is the action word. Angie, you gotta figure this stuff out for yourself. How you expect to learn anything? Bye, kiddo.

ANGELA. Thanks a lot, Stewart.

STEWIE. *(Going off.)* If you need any help, call me. *(A beat.)*

ANGELA. *(Excited.)* I should call you?

STEWIE. *(Further off.)* Yeah.

ANGELA. *(Calls.)* What's your phone number?

STEWIE. *(Calls back.)* Ask your brother. *(A beat.)*

ANGELA. *(Calls.)* Okay. See ya, Stewie!

End of Play

FIRST LOVE

FIRST LOVE

*Mickey and Cathy, eleven and nine, respectively, in the school
yard during lunchtime. Both are eating their lunches alone
and quietly. Mickey sneezes into his hand.*

MICKEY. Do you have a tissue?
CATHY. What?
MICKEY. Do you have a tissue or something?
CATHY. I have a napkin.
MICKEY. Can I have it?
CATHY. I only have one.
MICKEY Please. *(Pause.)*
CATHY. I'll give you half. *(She rips it, gives him half.)*
MICKEY. Thank you. *(Pause.)*
CATHY. You're welcome. *(Long pause.)*
MICKEY. Who do you have?
CATHY. What?
MICKEY. Who do you have? *(Pause.)*
CATHY. Mrs. Rubinstein.
MICKEY. Mrs. Rubinstein?
CATHY. Yeah.
MICKEY. The Mrs. Rubinstein with the red hair?
CATHY. Uh huh.
MICKEY. I had her. She makes you keep a separate science note-
book. Right?
CATHY. Yeah.
MICKEY. Don't worry. She gets nice. I had her. *(Pause.)* She's gonna
make you get a special notebook for vocabulary, too.
CATHY. I know. *(Pause.)*
MICKEY. Your mother's name is Sally, right?
CATHY. Yeah. *(Long silence.)*

MICKEY. My mother knows your mother. *(Pause.)* My mother's the vice president of the PTA. *(Pause.)* Is your mother in the PTA?
CATHY. I don't know.
MICKEY. Does your mother work?
CATHY. Yes.
MICKEY. My mother works, too. *(Pause.)* You ate at the coffee shoppe on Saturday. *(Pause.)* Didn't you eat at the coffee shoppe with your mother on Saturday?
CATHY. I think.
MICKEY. Yeah, you did. Your mother and my mother had lunch at the coffee shoppe on Saturday. Remember?
CATHY. I don't know.
MICKEY. Remember, there was a lady there with her son?
CATHY. Yeah. *(Pause.)*
MICKEY. That was me. We sat at your table. *(Long pause.)*
CATHY. *(She stands up.)* I have to go to the bathroom.
MICKEY. Do you know where it is? *(Pause. Cathy shakes her head "no.")* I'll show you.

End of Play

NEW YEAR'S EVE
AND
KIBBUTZ

NEW YEAR'S EVE and KIBBUTZ are two scenes from an abandoned play, *Heartbreaker*. It was commissioned by South Coast Repertory and developed at the Sundance Institute Playwrights' Conference in July 1989, where it featured Evan Handler as Jonathan, Daniel Jenkins as Bruce, Katherine Hiler as Paula and Kevin Kling as Yakov. After a workshop at SCR in November 1989, the play was shelved, but some of its scenes (not those included here) served as the basis for the play *Sight Unseen*.

NEW YEAR'S EVE

Lights up: The den of a middle-class house in Flatbush, Brooklyn. 1969. Wood paneling, well-nourished plants. Judaic ornaments dress the walls, with framed family photos. An electric menorah is fully lit in the window; its orange light and the bluish cast of the television illuminate two figures on the sofa: Jonathan and Paula, both fifteen going on sixteen. She is a frizzy-haired Earth Mother, braless in her father's shirt. She has been crying. The TV is tuned to a Fred Astaire–Ginger Rogers movie. Jonathan and Paula sit side by side, her hand stroking his inner thigh, his fondling her breast. They seem to be moving in slow motion while their eyes remain on the TV. Behind the sofa and to their left is an archway that leads to another part of the house; upstairs a party is going on. A bottle of wine is on the coffee table in front of them. Jonathan, already drunk, occasionally takes a swig to fortify his pursuit. This goes on for a while, until Bruce appears. He is the same age, slightly built; his hair is too short for him to pass as a hippie, although he wears jeans and wire-rimmed glasses. He stands in the doorway and secretly watches them in silence. After a long beat, he quietly sidles beside Paula and begins to fondle her thigh. Jonathan is unaware of his presence. Bruce, too, looks straight ahead at the TV, but gradually becomes engrossed in it.

BRUCE. *(Guessing.)* Top Hat?
JONATHAN. *(Surprised.)* Bruce! —
BRUCE. Charles Walters. Nineteen thirty … eight.
JONATHAN. Mark Sandrich, '35 —
BRUCE. Close.
JONATHAN. What do you want?
BRUCE. Everybody's wondering where you two went. I'm the

posse. It's T-minus ten minutes to the new decade. Don't you want to come up and watch the ball drop? *(Paula starts weeping again, takes the wine bottle from Jonathan and drinks.)* What's with Paula?

JONATHAN. Leave us alone.

BRUCE. Paula?

JONATHAN. She's depressed.

BRUCE. Why're you depressed?

JONATHAN. She's *depressed*. I'm *comforting* her.

BRUCE. *Com*forting her?! You call this *comf* — ?!

JONATHAN. Bruce…!

PAULA. I hate New Year's.

JONATHAN. *(To Bruce.)* Would you leave us alone please?

BRUCE. But don't you want to watch the little ball?

JONATHAN. We want to watch this.

PAULA. *(In utter seriousness.)* New Year's always does this to me. Worse than my birthday. It's something about seeing that new date on the newspaper the next morning. 1969 is gone forever. The sixties are gone forever. And there's nothing we can do to stop it. Nothing. We can't control it. It's bigger than us. It's like we're on a roller coaster and there's no stopping it. It's all going so fast all of a sudden, isn't it? We're getting old. *(She starts sobbing again.)*

JONATHAN. *(Gently amused.)* Paula, we're barely sixteen …

PAULA. Don't laugh at me!

JONATHAN. I'm not laughing!

PAULA. It's happening so fast all of a sudden! It is! It's accelerating! *(Bruce and Jonathan chortle.)* Don't laugh! Didn't this year go faster than last year? Didn't '68 go by faster than '67?

JONATHAN. Are you asking me?

PAULA. It's spinning out of our hands! Spinning and spinning, faster all the time! Our youth is disappearing! That's right, laugh at me. Soon we'll be in college, then we'll be married, then we'll be divorced, then we'll be dead. I don't want to die … *(She breaks down sobbing. Jonathan holds her and glares at Bruce to leave them alone. Pause. Bruce stays.)*

BRUCE. Are you still stoned from before? I think I am. Are you supposed to have like this amazing headache right here?

JONATHAN. *(Confidentially to Bruce, regarding Paula.)* She must be having her p —

114

PAULA. I am not! God!

JONATHAN. You said yourself, you only get like this when you have your —

PAULA. Like what? Emotional? You mean otherwise I'm not emotional? I need a hormone imbalance to —

JONATHAN. *(Over "imbalance to — ")* No, no … Shhh … Shut up. *(Suddenly looks queasy.)*

PAULA. What.

JONATHAN. I don't feel so good.

PAULA. Put your head down.

JONATHAN. *(Tries it.)* That's worse.

BRUCE. Are you gonna be sick?

JONATHAN. *(Trying to concentrate his nausea away.)* Just leave me alone.

PAULA. Are you?

JONATHAN. Leave me *alone!*

BRUCE. *(To Paula.)* He is.

JONATHAN. Bruce … *(Pause.)*

BRUCE. *(To Paula.)* You want to go up?

PAULA. *(Shakes her head no; to Jonathan.)* How do you feel now?

JONATHAN. Shhh …

PAULA. If you're gonna be sick, do me a favor and puke on my parents' bed. Do it right on the George Washington bedspread. *(Bruce changes the channel.)* Put that back.

BRUCE. I just wanted to see —

PAULA. Put it back. If you want to watch the ball drop — *(Bruce flips back to the movie.)* Thank you. *(Pause. To Jonathan.)* How ya doin'?

JONATHAN. Well, I wouldn't recommend kissing me right now … *(Bruce and Paula laugh; Jonathan doesn't realize how funny that sounded, and he laughs, too. For a moment, they're all convulsed with laughter but a new wave of nausea hits Jonathan and he stumbles to his feet.)* Uh-oh … *(Jonathan wavers a moment, then hurries through the doorway. Paula starts to go after him.)*

PAULA. Jonathan? … *(Bruce stops her by taking her hand. She looks at him for a beat.)*

BRUCE. Let him. *(A beat.)* He wouldn't want you watching him, you know … *(Pause. She joins him on the sofa. Silence, except for the*

115

TV, is broken by the sound of party revelers upstairs counting down from ten to the new year. Paula begins to cry again. Bruce watches her for a moment, not knowing what to do.) Paula?

PAULA. Nothing's the same anymore. My parents …

BRUCE. Shhh … *(Pause. He kisses her wet cheek, her brow, her eyes, her nose. They look at each other for a long beat as the offstage revelers hoot and cheer in celebration. Paula suddenly kisses him, long and deep. As quickly as she kissed him, she resumes watching the movie. Bruce is perplexed but watches also. Still crying, she moves her hand up his leg. He unbuttons her shirt and slips his hand inside as lights fade to black.)*

End of Play

KIBBUTZ

Lights up: a sun-drenched orchard on a kibbutz in the Israeli desert. 1972. Bruce, seventeen, wearing a bandanna around his head, cutoffs and a soiled white T-shirt, sits on the ground among several baskets full of peaches. He has made a writing surface of his army surplus shoulder bag, on which he composes a blue air-mail letter. Nearby is a small knapsack belonging to Jonathan. It is quiet. Birds pass overhead; Bruce looks up and tracks them, then writes about them in his letter. Soon, Yakov, a twenty-two-year-old, brawny, brown-skinned Israeli, shiny with sweat, runs very quickly past Bruce and offstage.

YAKOV. *(Without stopping.)* Hey! What are you *doing?!* Up up up! *(Yakov exits. Bruce watches him run in the distance, then returns to his letter. In a beat, Jonathan, also seventeen, wearing shorts and a Midwood High School T-shirt, enters. Flushed and perspired, he struggles with a bushel of freshly picked fruit and sets it down. Bruce hardly looks up from his writing.)*
JONATHAN. Who was *that?*
BRUCE. *(Still not looking up.) You* know.
JONATHAN. Yakov? *(No response.)* Bruce? Yakov?
BRUCE. I think. Yeah. *(Pause. Thick with tension.)*
JONATHAN. These Israelis. Boy. They're perfect machines. Strong to the finish. Yeah. A nation of Popeyes. All that matzoh and Coca-Cola. They don't sweat, these guys. No, they *glisten.* Like Kirk Douglas in *Spartacus.* Even the women. Incredible muscle definition.
BRUCE. *(Trying to concentrate on his letter.)* Jonathan …
JONATHAN. What. You're trying to write? Oooh, sorry. *(Jonathan stretches out. Very long pause.)* Who you writing to?
BRUCE. Paula.
JONATHAN. *(Sarcastically.)* Really? Again? That was a dumb

question. Boy is *she* gonna have some collection by the time we come home. All those air-letters … I run out of things to say on a *post*card. How could you be so full of things to say? *(Bruce looks annoyed again.)* I mean, how come you have so much to say and I have to write really big to fill a postcard? It's funny, that's all. *(Pause.)* What are you writing?

BRUCE. Jonathan …

JONATHAN. No, tell me: What are you *writing?* You don't have to *read* it to me or anything, I'm just curious. What types of things do you talk about?

BRUCE. What "types"?

JONATHAN. Yeah, you don't have to *read* it to me, I'm just curious.

BRUCE. I'm writing about our trip.

JONATHAN. Well, I figured as much.

BRUCE. Like a journal.

JONATHAN. Oh. Well. I write in my *journal* like a journal. So, in other words, instead of writing in a journal, you're making all these pithy observations to *Paula*. *("Pithy" angers Bruce.)* I mean, not "pithy" … *You* know: smart, clever. *(They look at one another for a long beat, then Bruce returns to his letter. Jonathan takes his sketchbook and a watercolor box out of his knapsack and sets up to sketch a landscape. Pause.)* You know, we used to tell each *other* our stupid theories of life. I mean, I still tell *you* and *then* I write it down in my little journal. *(Bruce looks up at him. Pause.)*

BRUCE. *(Gently, a bit guiltily.)* What. *(Meaning "What's the matter?")*

JONATHAN. *(A beat; quietly.)* Nothing. *(Jonathan and Bruce paint and write for a long beat.)* Say hi for me. *(Bruce doesn't respond.)* Bruce? Say hi for —

BRUCE. Yeah. *(Pause.)*

JONATHAN. What are you mad at *me* for?

BRUCE. Who's mad?!

JONATHAN. What are you mad at *me* for, *you're* the one who's always writing to fucking Paula, you never talk to *me* anymore …

BRUCE. *(Over "anymore.")* Well, aren't we sick of each other yet?, traveling around for five weeks?

JONATHAN. Are we? Gee. I guess we are. Gee, I —

YAKOV. *(Off.)* HEY! I don't believe you boys! *(Jonathan and Bruce shoot their sights toward the direction of the voice.)*

118

JONATHAN. Shit. It *is* Yakov … *(In a beat, Yakov approaches from the direction in which he ran. He is drinking from a canteen. He smiles always, but his tone is mocking, disingenuous.)*

YAKOV. Are you deaf?

BRUCE. Me?

YAKOV. Are you *stupid?*

BRUCE. Huh?

YAKOV. I told you to get up before. Didn't you see me when I ran by?

BRUCE. Uh-huh.

YAKOV. I told you to get *up,* back to work.

BRUCE. I thought you were kidding.

YAKOV. Why would I be kidding? You've come here to work?, or you've come here to play? *(To Jonathan.)* And what are *you* doing?

JONATHAN. Taking a break.

YAKOV. Oh. Tired?

JONATHAN. *(Tentatively.)* Yes.

YAKOV. You've been picking for two hours and you're tired?

JONATHAN. Since 8:30. It's almost twelve.

YAKOV. You're breaking my heart. I've been keeping an eye on you boys. A little rest here, a little break there … What a spectacle you boys are. This is not Miami Beach, I hate to break it to you. *(Yakov takes a long swig from his canteen, the water cascades down his neck and chest. He hands it to Jonathan.)*

JONATHAN. *(Surprised; as he takes it.)* Thanks. *(Bruce moves closer in anticipation; Jonathan tries to sip from it.)* It's empty.

YAKOV. *(Takes back the canteen.)* Oh, what a shame. *(Clicks his tongue.)* I feel sorry for you boys. Brooklyn boys. So pale. So delicate. Hands like pampered little girls'. I cringe for you when I see you working in the orchard. Slow-motion photography. Not even lunchtime and you're ready for your nap. Look at *you* and look at *me*: to think that we all, in the eyes of the world, we are all Jewish men. *(He touches his crotch lasciviously.)* Laughable. You don't know what hard work *is,* my friends … Boys … You American *children.* Your mommies and daddies send you over on jets, for what? To *ed*ucate you? No, I'm *ask*ing you. To turn you into good little Zionists, what? Cultural exchange? What is the fascination? I don't understand. This is, what, an alternative to summer camp for you?

Arts and crafts? I see you have your little sketchbook. *(Reaches for it; Jonathan resists.)* Please. *(Jonathan hesitates, then gives it to Yakov, who looks through it.)* Oh, so you are a good little artist. Look at that: the orchard! I see! *(Flips pages; a tad mocking.)* Our cows, yes! Very good! Look at that: the Administration Building. Very talented. *(Returns the book to Jonathan.)* This is my *life,* you know, this is my *home.* We kibbutzniks are not here for your entertainment. This is not a country club for rich Jewish children. I am not the boy who cleans the pool and changes your linens.

JONATHAN. I'm not "rich."

YAKOV. You're not? Forgive me. I don't mean rich. I mean … spoiled. Yes. Safe. You see, we go on in this fashion long after you fly home on your 747s. We remain. We are just an outing for you. Something to snap pictures of. This is not kibbutz-Disneyland where you ride the amusements and go home smiling. You have to participate. On our terms. You are guests. But you are the kind who expect only to be served and never rise to clean the dishes.

JONATHAN. I washed the dishes last night.

YAKOV. So you did. You know what I mean. You aren't ignorant. What do you know of survival? What do you know of death? In the Six Day War, seventeen years old, I fought. How old are you?

JONATHAN. *(Ashamed.)* That age.

YAKOV. *(Laughs, then.)* And where were *you* in '67? Dragging yourself off to Hebrew lessons when you'd've rather been playing baseball? I was fighting for your right to exist. *(Pause. He touches Jonathan's face strangely, menacingly, sexually. A beat.)* Back to work, boys. *(He starts to go off, snatching a peach from the basket as he goes. Jonathan touches his cheek and looks at his fingers, as if he's checking for blood. He's shaken by the encounter. To dispel the tension, Bruce touches Jonathan's face in a lame attempt at a joke.)*

BRUCE. "Back to work, boys … " *(Jonathan is not amused; he pushes Bruce's hand away.)*

JONATHAN. Fuck *you,* Bruce!

BRUCE. *(Now also very upset.)* Well, fuck *you!* (In a flash, they're pushing and punching each other furiously. It's very heated and very quick. In the midst of the skirmish, Jonathan violently grabs Bruce's letter.)* Jonathan! Jonathan, give me … Give it back! *(Jonathan crumples the letter and throws it to the ground. They separate, out of breath, their*

adrenaline rushing wildly. Bruce retrieves the balled-up letter and smooths it out. Jonathan watches him for a beat.)
JONATHAN. Bruce? Brucie? I'm sorry, Bruce ... *(Bruce ignores him as he gathers his things.)* Bruce? *(Bruce starts to go, walking past him; Jonathan reaches for his friend's shoulder.)* Hey ... *(Bruce evades Jonathan's touch. Jonathan watches him exit. He watches him walk farther into the distance, then calls to him at the top of his lungs.)* Brucie?! *(Fade out.)*

End of Play

PROPERTY AND SOUND EFFECTS LISTS

Nocturne

PROPERTY LIST
Basin and pitcher
Stuffed rabbit (BOY)
Doll house, dolls (BOY)
Doctor's bag (MONSTER)
Toys (MONSTERS)
Dagger (MONSTER)
Candle (FATHER)
Blanket (FATHER)
Translucent orb (BOY)

SOUND EFFECTS
Wind
Thunder
Child calling
Fluttering of wings
Knocking

Luna Park

PROPERTY LIST
Book (DELMORE)
Dishes (ROSE)
Knife (ROSE)
Garbage can (ROSE)
Handkerchief (ROSE)
Phonograph (DELMORE)
Record (DELMORE)
Flashlight (USHER)
Loose change (HARRY)
Napkin (GRANDFATHER)
Watch (HARRY)
Cigars (HARRY, GRANDFATHER)
Lighters (HARRY, GRANDFATHER)

Dog leash (DELMORE)
Bag of crumbs (DELMORE)
Bag of peanuts (HARRY)
Restaurant table settings, glasses (HARRY, ROSE)
Pitcher of water (DELMORE)
Dessert menus (DELMORE)
Slices of chocolate cake and cheesecake (DELMORE)
Tray, dish of sherbet, two glasses of tea (DELMORE)
Napkins, silverware (DELMORE)
Camera on tripod (DELMORE)
Bouquet of artificial flowers (DELMORE)
Chair (DELMORE)
Crystal ball, cloth (DELMORE)
Quarter (HARRY)
Box of popcorn (DELMORE)
Broom, dust pan (USHER)
Place settings, glasses, teabags (ROSE)
Newspaper (ROSE)
Tea kettle (ROSE)
Sewing basket, needle, thread (ROSE)

SOUND EFFECTS
Recording of a Haydn string quartet
Needle skipping on phonograph
Breathing
Organ music
Movie projector running
Doorbell chiming
Rustling leaves
Ocean
Wind and waves
Calliope music
Distant violin
Romantic music
Crescendo of romantic music
Radio
Tea kettle whistling

Misadventure

SOUND EFFECTS
Car starting

I Don't Know What I'm Doing

PROPERTY LIST
Envelope, letter (NANCY)
Bag (NANCY)
Slice of cake wrapped in tinfoil (NANCY)

Father and Son

PROPERTY LIST
Checkbook (FATHER, SON)
Check ledger (FATHER, SON)

Death in the Family

PROPERTY LIST
Telephones (MICKEY, IRVING)

Homework

PROPERTY LIST
Homework (ANGELA)
Pen (ANGELA)

First Love

PROPERTY LIST
Lunches (CATHY, MICKEY)
Napkin (CATHY, MICKEY)

New Year's Eve

PROPERTY LIST
Bottle of wine (JONATHAN)
Television (BRUCE)

SOUND EFFECTS
Party noises
Party revelers counting down to the new year
Hooting and cheering

Kibbutz

PROPERTY LIST
Shoulder bag (BRUCE)
Air-mail stationery, pen (BRUCE)
Baskets of peaches (JONATHAN)
Knapsack (JONATHAN)
Sketchbook, watercolor box (JONATHAN)
Canteen (YAKOV)

NEW PLAYS

★ **THE EXONERATED by Jessica Blank and Erik Jensen.** Six interwoven stories paint a picture of an American criminal justice system gone horribly wrong and six brave souls who persevered to survive it. "The #1 play of the year...intense and deeply affecting..." *–NY Times.* "Riveting. Simple, honest storytelling that demands reflection." *–A.P.* "Artful and moving...pays tribute to the resilience of human hearts and minds." *–Variety.* "Stark...riveting...cunningly orchestrated." *–The New Yorker.* "Hard-hitting, powerful, and socially relevant." *–Hollywood Reporter.* [7M, 3W] ISBN: 0-8222-1946-8

★ **STRING FEVER by Jacquelyn Reingold.** Lily juggles the big issues: turning forty, artificial insemination and the elusive scientific Theory of Everything in this Off-Broadway comedy hit. "Applies the elusive rules of string theory to the conundrums of one woman's love life. Think *Sex and the City* meets *Copenhagen.*" *–NY Times.* "A funny offbeat and touching look at relationships...an appealing romantic comedy populated by oddball characters." *–NY Daily News.* "Where kooky, zany, and madcap meet...whimsically winsome." *–NY Magazine.* "STRING FEVER will have audience members happily stringing along." *–TheaterMania.com.* "Reingold's language is surprising, inventive, and unique." *–nytheatre.com.* "...[a] whimsical comic voice." *–Time Out.* [3M, 3W (doubling)] ISBN: 0-8222-1952-2

★ **DEBBIE DOES DALLAS adapted by Erica Schmidt, composed by Andrew Sherman, conceived by Susan L. Schwartz.** A modern morality tale told as a comic musical of tragic proportions as the classic film is brought to the stage. "A scream! A saucy, tongue-in-cheek romp." *–The New Yorker.* "Hilarious! DEBBIE manages to have it all: beauty, brains and a great sense of humor!" *–Time Out.* "Shamelessly silly, shrewdly self-aware and proud of being naughty. Great fun!" *–NY Times.* "Racy and raucous, a lighthearted, fast-paced thoroughly engaging and hilarious send-up." *–NY Daily News.* [3M, 5W] ISBN: 0-8222-1955-7

★ **THE MYSTERY PLAYS by Roberto Aguirre-Sacasa.** Two interrelated one acts, loosely based on the tradition of the medieval mystery plays. "... stylish, spine-tingling...Mr. Aguirre-Sacasa uses standard tricks of horror stories, borrowing liberally from masters like Kafka, Lovecraft, Hitchcock...But his mastery of the genre is his own...irresistible." *–NY Times.* "Undaunted by the special-effects limitations of theatre, playwright and *Marvel* comic-book writer Roberto Aguirre-Sacasa maps out some creepy twilight zones in THE MYSTERY PLAYS, an engaging, related pair of one acts...The theatre may rarely deliver shocks equivalent to, say, *Dawn of the Dead,* but Aguirre-Sacasa's work is fine compensation." *–Time Out.* [4M, 2W] ISBN: 0-8222-2038-5

★ **THE JOURNALS OF MIHAIL SEBASTIAN by David Auburn.** This epic one-man play spans eight tumultuous years and opens a uniquely personal window on the Romanian Holocaust and the Second World War. "Powerful." *–NY Times.* "[THE JOURNALS OF MIHAIL SEBASTIAN] allows us to glimpse the idiosyncratic effects of that awful history on one intelligent, pragmatic, recognizably real man..." *–NY Newsday.* [3M, 5W] ISBN: 0-8222-2006-7

★ **LIVING OUT by Lisa Loomer.** The story of the complicated relationship between a Salvadoran nanny and the Anglo lawyer she works for. "A stellar new play. Searingly funny." *–The New Yorker.* "Both generous and merciless, equally enjoyable and disturbing." *–NY Newsday.* "A bitingly funny new comedy. The plight of working mothers is explored from two pointedly contrasting perspectives in this sympathetic, sensitive new play." *–Variety.* [2M, 6W] ISBN: 0-8222-1994-8

DRAMATISTS PLAY SERVICE, INC.
440 Park Avenue South, New York, NY 10016 212-683-8960 Fax 212-213-1539
postmaster@dramatists.com www.dramatists.com

NEW PLAYS

★ **MATCH by Stephen Belber.** Mike and Lisa Davis interview a dancer and choreographer about his life, but it is soon evident that their agenda will either ruin or inspire them—and definitely change their lives forever. "Prolific laughs and ear-to-ear smiles." *–NY Magazine.* "Uproariously funny, deeply moving, enthralling theater. Stephen Belber's MATCH has great beauty and tenderness, and abounds in wit." *–NY Daily News.* "Three and a half out of four stars." *–USA Today.* "A theatrical steeplechase that leads straight from outrageous bitchery to unadorned, heartfelt emotion." *–Wall Street Journal.* [2M, 1W] ISBN: 0-8222-2020-2

★ **HANK WILLIAMS: LOST HIGHWAY by Randal Myler and Mark Harelik.** The story of the beloved and volatile country-music legend Hank Williams, featuring twenty-five of his most unforgettable songs. "[LOST HIGHWAY has] the exhilarating feeling of Williams on stage in a particular place on a particular night…serves up classic country with the edges raw and the energy hot…By the end of the play, you've traveled on a profound emotional journey: LOST HIGHWAY transports its audience and communicates the inspiring message of the beauty and richness of Williams' songs…forceful, clear-eyed, moving, impressive." *–Rolling Stone.* "…honors a very particular musical talent with care and energy… smart, sweet, poignant." *–NY Times.* [7M, 3W] ISBN: 0-8222-1985-9

★ **THE STORY by Tracey Scott Wilson.** An ambitious black newspaper reporter goes against her editor to investigate a murder and finds the *best* story…but at what cost? "A singular new voice…deeply emotional, deeply intellectual, and deeply musical…" *–The New Yorker.* "…a conscientious and absorbing new drama…" *–NY Times.* "…a riveting, tough-minded drama about race, reporting and the truth…" *–A.P.* "… a stylish, attention-holding script that ends on a chilling note that will leave viewers with much to talk about." *–Curtain Up.* [2M, 7W (doubling, flexible casting)] ISBN: 0-8222-1998-0

★ **OUR LADY OF 121st STREET by Stephen Adly Guirgis.** The body of Sister Rose, beloved Harlem nun, has been stolen, reuniting a group of life-challenged childhood friends who square off as they wait for her return. "A scorching and dark new comedy… Mr. Guirgis has one of the finest imaginations for dialogue to come along in years." *–NY Times.* "Stephen Guirgis may be the best playwright in America under forty." *–NY Magazine.* [8M, 4W] ISBN: 0-8222-1965-4

★ **HOLLYWOOD ARMS by Carrie Hamilton and Carol Burnett.** The coming-of-age story of a dreamer who manages to escape her bleak life and follow her romantic ambitions to stardom. Based on Carol Burnett's bestselling autobiography, *One More Time.* "…pure theatre and pure entertainment…" *–Talkin' Broadway.* "…a warm, fuzzy evening of theatre." *–BrodwayBeat.com.* "…chuckles and smiles of recognition or surprise flow naturally…a remarkable slice of life." *–TheatreScene.net.* [5M, 5W, 1 girl] ISBN: 0-8222-1959-X

★ **INVENTING VAN GOGH by Steven Dietz.** A haunting and hallucinatory drama about the making of art, the obsession to create and the fine line that separates truth from myth. "Like a van Gogh painting, Dietz's story is a gorgeous example of excess—one that remakes reality with broad, well-chosen brush strokes. At evening's end, we're left with the author's resounding opinions on art and artifice, and provoked by his constant query into which is greater: van Gogh's art or his violent myth." *–Phoenix New Times.* "Dietz's writing is never simple. It is always brilliant. Shaded, compressed, direct, lucid—he frames his subject with a remarkable understanding of painting as a physical experience." *–Tucson Citizen.* [4M, 1W] ISBN: 0-8222-1954-9

DRAMATISTS PLAY SERVICE, INC.
440 Park Avenue South, New York, NY 10016 212-683-8960 Fax 212-213-1539
postmaster@dramatists.com www.dramatists.com

NEW PLAYS

★ **INTIMATE APPAREL by Lynn Nottage.** The moving and lyrical story of a turn-of-the-century black seamstress whose gifted hands and sewing machine are the tools she uses to fashion her dreams from the whole cloth of her life's experiences. "…Nottage's play has a delicacy and eloquence that seem absolutely right for the time she is depicting…" –*NY Daily News.* "…thoughtful, affecting…The play offers poignant commentary on an era when the cut and color of one's dress—and of course, skin—determined whom one could and could not marry, sleep with, even talk to in public." –*Variety.* [2M, 4W] ISBN: 0-8222-2009-1

★ **BROOKLYN BOY by Donald Margulies.** A witty and insightful look at what happens to a writer when his novel hits the bestseller list. "The characters are beautifully drawn, the dialogue sparkles…" –*nytheatre.com.* "Few playwrights have the mastery to smartly investigate so much through a laugh-out-loud comedy that combines the vintage subject matter of successful writer-returning-to-ethnic-roots with the familiar mid-life crisis." –*Show Business Weekly.* [4M, 3W] ISBN: 0-8222-2074-1

★ **CROWNS by Regina Taylor.** Hats become a springboard for an exploration of black history and identity in this celebratory musical play. "Taylor pulls off a Hat Trick: She scores thrice, turning CROWNS into an artful amalgamation of oral history, fashion show, and musical theater…" –*TheatreMania.com.* "…wholly theatrical…Ms. Taylor has created a show that seems to arise out of spontaneous combustion, as if a bevy of department-store customers simultaneously decided to stage a revival meeting in the changing room." –*NY Times.* [1M, 6W (2 musicians)] ISBN: 0-8222-1963-8

★ **EXITS AND ENTRANCES by Athol Fugard.** The story of a relationship between a young playwright on the threshold of his career and an aging actor who has reached the end of his. "[Fugard] can say more with a single line than most playwrights convey in an entire script…Paraphrasing the title, it's safe to say this drama, making its memorable entrance into our consciousness, is unlikely to exit as long as a theater exists for exceptional work." –*Variety.* "A thought-provoking, elegant and engrossing new play…" –*Hollywood Reporter.* [2M] ISBN: 0-8222-2041-5

★ **BUG by Tracy Letts.** A thriller featuring a pair of star-crossed lovers in an Oklahoma City motel facing a bug invasion, paranoia, conspiracy theories and twisted psychological motives. "…obscenely exciting…top-flight craftsmanship. Buckle up and brace yourself…" –*NY Times.* "…[a] thoroughly outrageous and thoroughly entertaining play…the possibility of enemies, real and imagined, to squash has never been more theatrical." –*A.P.* [3M, 2W] ISBN: 0-8222-2016-4

★ **THOM PAIN (BASED ON NOTHING) by Will Eno.** An ordinary man muses on childhood, yearning, disappointment and loss, as he draws the audience into his last-ditch plea for empathy and enlightenment. "It's one of those treasured nights in the theater—treasured nights anywhere, for that matter—that can leave you both breathless with exhilaration and…in a puddle of tears." –*NY Times.* "Eno's words…are familiar, but proffered in a way that is constantly contradictory to our expectations. Beckett is certainly among his literary ancestors." –*nytheatre.com.* [1M] ISBN: 0-8222-2076-8

★ **THE LONG CHRISTMAS RIDE HOME by Paula Vogel.** Past, present and future collide on a snowy Christmas Eve for a troubled family of five. "…[a] lovely and hauntingly original family drama…a work that breathes so much life into the theater." –*Time Out.* "…[a] delicate visual feast…" –*NY Times.* "…brutal and lovely…the overall effect is magical." –*NY Newsday.* [3M, 3W] ISBN: 0-8222-2003-2

DRAMATISTS PLAY SERVICE, INC.
440 Park Avenue South, New York, NY 10016 212-683-8960 Fax 212-213-1539
postmaster@dramatists.com www.dramatists.com